Normative Political Science

An Exciting New Way to do Poli Sci Research

William J. Kelleher, PhD

Empathic Science Institute

Los Angeles, California

Empathic Science Institute

2158 La Canada Crest Dr ste 4

La Canada, CA 91011-1920

First Printing: August 2023

USA

ISBN: 978-0-9773717-3-0

Cover by Guy

To Henry T. Gardner, my philosophy teacher. He introduced me to Hartman, and advised me to read Polanyi. I later discovered Easton, and the seeds of synthesis were planted.

Table of Contents

Introduction

As you know, the title of this book is "Normative Political Science." At first this may seem like an oxymoron. A reader might wonder if the author really understands what he is saying. Everyone knows that "norms" are about value judgments, and that "science" eschews value judgments in favor of just dealing in factual matters. In other words, one may think that science focuses on "what is," not on "what ought to be."

The truth is that political science, like all other natural and social science organizations, has a plethora of rules and norms. These include, for instance, the requirements to become a member of a scientific organization. Nobody can just come in off the street. In most of these organizations, PhDs are the most welcomed.

Once in, there are norms for behavior as a professional. These can include how one acts in society, on campus, and especially how one carries out research. In political science, for example, a teacher who campaigns for office in the classroom, or advocates for her or his favorite political philosophy, will soon be confronted by the APSA Ethics Committee and The Ad Hoc Committee on Membership Revocation.[1] The same result will likely follow in cases of professors and teachers who bully students, or engage in sexual harassment, etc.

The way research is conducted is a matter of great concern within the political science profession. Anyone who falsifies evidence in a research report, for example, risks being publicly censured and possibly booted out of the profession. But the term "norms" governs much more than boorish and dishonest behavior. Norms can guide what is treated as acceptable research assumptions and methods. In other words, "good work" in political science.[2]

In "The Normative Structure of Science," first published in 1942, Robert K. Merton distinguished "the ethos of science"[3] from its professional ethics and the norms governing best methodological practices. The study was path breaking, in part, because the positivist myth still prevailed at the time that "science" was "value free," and only concerned with facts. Indeed, this myth still lingers among those who pay little attention to the sociology of science.

Focused mainly on the natural sciences, Merton observed that "science" is a collaborative enterprise, and that scientists, no matter their field of specialty, actually followed and enforced an identifiable set of rules, or norms, which they had established for themselves over the many generations during which the institution of science had been developing. He noted that this ethos is generally shaped in ways that are meant to facilitate the realization of the institution's goals. In Merton's view, "The [primary] institutional goal of science is the extension of certified knowledge."[4]

The norms, or ethos, that Merton had in mind include such noble ideas as the free sharing of information, putting the scientific community's interest in producing reliable knowledge above any national self-interest in gaining advantage, the willingness to have one's research findings subjected to the scrutiny of colleagues (i.e., peer review), and to follow the practice of free thinking skepticism, rather than insisting on a dogmatic assertion of principles, such as can be seen in religion.

Merton comments that other "sentiments embodied in the ethos of science [include] intellectual honesty, integrity, [and] impersonality."[5]

Merton notes that these "imperatives, transmitted by precept and example and reinforced by sanctions are in varying degrees internalized by the scientist, thus fashioning his scientific conscience."[6] Students in graduate programs, and young professionals, learn the rules of science by instruction, but they also internalize the ethos through their exposure to models, such as teachers and mentors. Merton cites the sociologist, Albert Bayet, who wrote that this ethos "is implied in the very existence of science."[7]

As institutional imperatives for science, these norms persist, in part, not only because they are enforced by peer pressure and sanctions for breeches, but because among scientists "they are believed right and good. They are moral as well as technical prescriptions."[8] These are the norms which guide the attitudes and behavior of individuals who identify as "scientists."[9]

Recent surveys of scientists show that a very high percentage of them, both in natural science and social science, continue to subscribe to these norms. Reports of belief in some of the Mertonian norms ranged from 73% to 91%.[10]

The Normative Political Science paradigm can fit right in with the ethos of science described by Merton. However, as we will show in the text, the methodological principles of Normative Political Science are offered as a *replacement* for the dominant positivistic notions of how to conduct research in political science. The positivist's norms include defining "science" as centered on hypotheses testing, replication, objectivity, value neutrality, etc. Why these methodological ideals, or norms, are unacceptable to Normative Political Science will be explained thoroughly.

What is Normative Political Science?

At this point, the reader might ask, with what would the Normative Political Science paradigm replace the current positivist paradigm?

My reply is that the Normative Political Science paradigm consists of what I call the "Easton-Hartman Synthesis." That includes Easton's core writings on his theory of the political system. This theory will be explained in Chapter One. We will see that Easton understood himself as writing about a way to do empirical research so as to understand and explain the meanings political actors were, or are, acting upon as members of a system. I call this "explanatory political science."

The Hartman part uses Easton's theory of the political system, not as an interpretive framework for understanding and explanation, but as a clearly defined *standard* by which to assess how well a particular political system is working. I call this "evaluative political science." Hartman's addition, then, is the thesis that the operation of a system can be evaluated by comparing its actual behavior with the ideals implied in the theory of the political system. This is something even Easton had not realized is possible.

Easton came close to this new understanding of the use of his theory of the political system when he stressed in his writings that he distinguished between two kinds of political system. One is the behavioral political system. That is, the actual interactions of political actors on the ground. This is the typical subject of political science. The other kind of political system is the conceptual framework, ideal, or definition of the political system. In other words, the idea of the thing, and the thing itself, are distinct and not to be confused.

Something else that Easton's distinction makes possible, but which he did not see himself, is that if there is a distinct behavioral political system operating in real life, where did it come from? How did the first behavioral political system come into being on this planet? Addressing that question will be the aim of Chapter Two. This will draw on the findings of paleoanthropology and evolutionary biology.[11]

Then, in Chapter Three, we will return to the other half of the two sides of Easton's theory of the political system. That is, the Hartman insight into the use of the theory as a "norm," a way to assess the operational goodness of any particular political system. After explaining that, we will move on to Chapter Four and apply what we have learned to assessing the operational goodness of the Chinese political system. The reader will see that the potential for new knowledge this paradigm makes possible is the reason why this is truly an exciting new way of doing political science research.

Because this research method is so new, some changes in the way the American political science profession is organized will be necessary. We will adapt Easton's vision for the organization of the profession to incorporate evaluative political science. The dominant view that "science" is unable to assess goodness will have to go by the wayside. New ideas of "good work," and of research worthy of support and publication, will have to be instituted to accommodate the new political science. As will be discussed in Chapter Five, there may be some resistance within the profession for the proponents of Normative Political Science to overcome.

In the Conclusion we will consider the art of diagnosing the causes of whatever below par performances are revealed when assessing the operational goodness of a political system. Upon diagnosis, of course, the way is opened for recommending remedial policies. This is another change that Normative Political Science will bring to the profession. Political science has the potential to make of itself the center of political wisdom, looked up to by society as the primary source of problem solving policies. As the reader will see, Normative Political Science will enable the profession to realize that potential.

Endnotes

1. The APSA Ethics Guide says that it is intended to provide a clear statement of ethical principles for political scientists—including faculty, students, administrators and practitioners. The Ethics Guide can be found at https://apsanet.org/ethics

2. For a short discussion of different ideas about "good work" in political science see, Kelleher, William. A Model Discipline, and How "Good Work" Hurts Political Science. Perspectives on Politics. Volume 13, Issue 2. June 2015. 446 – 448. DOI: https://doi.org/10.1017/S1537592715000262

For a more in-depth analysis of how the worship of the H-D model of "science" degrades the relevance and public respect of our profession see my Western Political Science Association paper, "The Clarke and Primo Liberating Conception of Good Work in Political Science." (free) at,

https://www.academia.edu/10417226/The_Clarke_and_Primo_Liberating_Conception_of_Good_Work_in_Political_Science

3. Merton, Robert K. 1973,1942. "The Normative Structure of Science," in Merton, Robert K. (ed.), *The Sociology of Science: Theoretical and Empirical Investigations*. Chicago: University of Chicago Press. 267–278, 258. (Free copy of Merton's essay as a chapter from the cited book at, https://law.unimelb.edu.au/__data/assets/pdf_file/0005/3609203/1c-Merton-The-Normative-Structure-of-Science.pdf Accessed April 20, 2023.)

4. Other terms for this aim can include "validated knowledge," or, Easton's term, "reliable knowledge."

5. Merton, ibid., 259.

6. Ibid., 269.

7. Ibid., 269.

8. Ibid., 270.

9. Ibid., 268.

10. Anderson, Melissa S., et al. "Extending the Mertonian Norms: Scientists' Subscription to Norms of Research." The Journal of Higher Education, vol. 81 no. 3, 2010, 366-393, 387. doi:10.1353/jhe.0.0095. (Free read online or download at, https://www.ncbi.nlm.nih.gov/pmc/articles/PMC2995462/.) Accessed April 20, 2023. Also see Pub Med, https://pubmed.ncbi.nlm.nih.gov/21132074/ with lists for "Similar Articles" and "Cited by."

Cf. Hillmert, Steffen. The "Normative Structure" of Social Science: Merton's Ideas as a Story of Success and Side Effects. Serendipities. June 2021 (2): 42–62. DOI:10.7146/serendipities.v6i2.130014 42 Free online read at,

11. Easton wrote a review of anthropological literature for the years 1956-1957. But this literature was about contemporary indigenous societies, rather than about society in the distant past. And, because none of the studies he reviewed used his concept of the political system to explain the political behavior of indigenous peoples, he concluded that no sub-field worthy of the name "political anthropology" yet exists. 210f. Easton, David. "Political Anthropology." 210-260. 1959. In *Biennial Review of Anthropology*. Bernard Siegel (ed). Stanford: Stanford University Press 1959. Text available for free reading at,
https://archive.org/details/biennialreviewof033489mbp/page/n1/mode/2up
The full text available to copy for free is at,
https://archive.org/stream/biennialreviewof033489mbp/biennialreviewof0334 89mbp_djvu.txt

Chapter One:

Easton's Axiom: The Wellspring of Normative Political Science

Introduction

Historian of the political science profession, John Gunnell, has observed that David Easton's main work, *The Political System*, "has now become somewhat a prisoner of the perspectives that have subsequently informed its interpretive history."[12] Despite its popularity, he questions whether the book has ever been truly understood, and notes that, even "after two generations," the "actual text has never been fully and carefully analyzed."[13] Therefore, "it is worthwhile reexamining in detail the structure of the argument and determining its place in Easton's path to the formulation of a systems analysis of political life."[14] He adds that given the passage of time since the book's first publication in 1953, it "is in some respects possible today to understand the book better than it was understood in the 1950s, and it may be possible to understand the author better than he understood himself."[15] Gunnell, then, proceeds to render an erudite account of the historical context of Easton's famous classic text, *The Political System.*

While the instant paper has benefitted from Gunnell's learned elucidation of Easton's main work, this essay undertakes the same "reexamining" project as Gunnell, but from an entirely different point of view. This exegeses of the systematic political theory Easton introduces in *The Political System,* and spells out in succeeding texts, focuses not on its history, but on its singularity; that is, its creative origins, intentionality, and interconnectedness.[16] The common categorizations of Easton as a "positivist," or a "behavioralist," obscure the uniqueness of his political theory, which will be elucidated here.[17]

The Need for a Systematic Theory of Politics

Surveying the field in mid-20th century, David Easton observed that political science primarily lacks "a conceptual framework or systematic theory to give meaning, coherence, and direction to ongoing research."[18] In his most prominent work, *The Political System*, he writes, "In political science there has been little deliberate effort to formulate a conceptual framework for the whole field."[19] The problem he undertakes, then, is that of "defining political science," and thus to "define the core of the field."[20] This is Easton's heroic mission.

Easton regretted what he saw as the "flight from scientific reason, especially in the area of political knowledge."[21] His discussion of "science" shows that he understands the concept broadly as an organized frame of reference with an empirical orientation, a defined subject matter (in this case, "politics"), and a systematic approach to seeking causal knowledge about the subject. Easton's theory of "political knowledge" may be his least appreciated and most surprising contribution to political science; therefore, this chapter will center on its explication.

Easton envisions science as the apex of human reason.[22] He notes that he is far from the first to search for a science of politics, but he is intent upon pursuing that goal. To have a science of politics, Easton argues, political scientists must begin with a clear idea of what "politics" is. "Where does the political begin and end, and how is it distinguishable if at all, from other kinds of data that we call economic, sociological, psychological, and so on."[23] Such a theoretical demarcation is needed "to identify the significant variables necessary to explain political activities and to show their interrelations."[24]

Hyperfactualism

Easton found that one of the consequences for political science of lacking a theory of the field, or field theory, was the pervasive condition he called "hyperfactualism." Rather dramatically he declared, the "American political scientist is born free but is everywhere in chains, tied to a hyperfactual past."[25]

Hyperfactual political science assumes that "science" consists exclusively of objective and detached fact gathering.[26] But, in Easton's view, this assumption about the nature of science is way off the mark. In the natural sciences, such as biology, physics, or chemistry the field's subject matter is understood, and this understanding provides guidance to researchers within the field. It is absurd to think that researchers act with a blank slate of a mind. Instead, the selection of an event for study "is made in the light of a frame of reference that fixes the order and relevance of the facts."[27] This field theory serves as an interpretive framework that guides research and gives particular facts, out of the whole, their special significance. Without such "theoretical assumptions

… it would be impossible for them to select meaningful facts."[28]

Thus, no matter the reasons for the pursuit of research, it is "scientific" if it is conducted with a systematic approach and from within an orderly "frame of reference."[29] His concept of science also includes an understanding of verifying or validating the fruits of research, which will be discussed further in a moment. And, as we will see, these principles inform Easton's theory of political knowledge.

Below the Level of Theory

But, without a systematic theory to guide their selections of topics and related facts, how were political science researchers in the past able to write anything about politics? Indeed, how could separate fields of social science, such as political science and psychology, even develop without theoretical guidance?

In Easton's interpretation, it was a pioneer's subjective understanding of "the intrinsic logic" of each field in the social sciences that lead to their development as separate areas of research.[30] From his reading of history, Easton had learned that "sciences do not arise capriciously."[31] "Some process of selection does take place."[32] Easton notes that specializations in the social sciences have not developed as mere "historical accident," but by "a rationale of their own." Out of the complexity of "social life," leading writers selected clusters of interactions for study.[33] Original thinkers in various fields linked together sets of recurring issues, problems, challenges, observations, and questions, often led by an *intuitive sense* that the issues were related.[34] Writers who shared overlapping intellectual passions helped develop specialized fields of social science.

For instance, psychology was pulled together, or socially constructed, by writers who shared the intellectual passion to understand individual behavior.[35] By the subject matter they put together they distinguished their field from other social sciences, such as economics, political science, or geography. Easton points out that those writers intuited a kind of "logic of the situation." Those who made careful studies of particular aspects of society understood and shared certain "key questions" which helped to define their professions. Unarticulated tacit factors, such as a personal sense of the subject and intuition, served as research guides in lieu of a defined conceptual framework. Thus, leading figures paved the way, following their own *inner sense* of the subject matter.

For Easton, political science in particular, has risen largely out of the personal interest of pioneering researchers in understanding how policy for society is made and implemented. In the absence of a systematic theory defining the field of political science, "most students of political life do feel quite instinctively that research into the political aspects of life does differ from inquiry into any other [aspect of social life]."[36] "Quite instinctively" political science researchers select some kinds of facts rather than others.[37] Among Easton's most admired pioneering political scientists is V. O. Key, in part because he had a "feel for politics," which distinguished his writings from the more crude hyperfactualists.[38]

Common Sense

Apart from instinct and feel, some political scientists have used "common sense" notions of what is *political* as their implicit orientation to the subject. Common sense understands politics to include politicking – "maneuvering for position and power."[39] It also understands politics as "an activity related in some vague way to problems of government or the making of policy for the whole society," and involving disputes "over the policies accepted as authoritative for the society."[40] Easton notes that one of the characteristics distinguishing science from common sense is the "deliberate attempt to bring to the surface what common sense leaves permanently concealed."[41] Thus, Easton wants "to raise these assumptions to the point of consciousness for the purposes of careful examination."[42] Common sense can be misleading or mistaken, and can vary among researchers, so an explicit field theory can center collective attention, and critically discern the relevant knowledge from writings based on differing notions of common sense, intuition, etc.[43]

The Axiom and Emergent System

Aspiring to make the field more scientific, Easton asks how the conduct of political science research can be made more *rational* than by following various forms of preconscious intuition. Many of those who doubt the efficacy of scientific rationality have been relying on the guidance of such nebulous factors as feel, common sense, instinct, etc. But, as noted, this can lead to difficulties in a profession for several reasons, not the least of which is that various writers might not share the same preconceptual feelings. Thus, Easton will attempt to free the profession from its reliance on vague tacit notions by explicitly defining the core of the field in a way that both appeals to reason and can be criticized rationally. He begins this effort by presenting his basic axiom for political science.

Now familiar to political scientists, Easton's axiom may fairly be stated that "politics," the subject of political science, *is that human behavior undertaken in relation to the authoritative allocation of values for a society.*[44] This axiom is meant to, among other things, "sum up our common sense conception of politics."[45] Once its key terms are defined, which Easton does, the axiom raises the vagaries of undefined intuitive sensitivities to a clear conceptual level. Because it is in an articulated form, practitioners in the field will be able to rationally criticize the axiom. As we will see, Easton understood his axiom as having implications for not only the scope, but also the methods of the field.[46]

From the axiom guided observations of the complex behavior of individual humans on the ground, which constitute political life, the vision of a persistent political system *emerges.*[47] As Easton writes, with the axiom guiding observation it becomes clear that "political life constitutes a concrete political system which is an aspect of the whole social system." [48] This insight calls attention to another fault of hyperfactualism, namely that it conceals "from students of political life the need to view the political system as a whole."[49]

For Easton, such terms as "political life" and "political process" are general references to the same subject matter as the "political system;" namely, all those human interactions undertaken in relation to the authoritative allocation of values for a society. The "political system" entails "all those kinds of activities involved in the formulation and execution of social policy;" i.e., "the policy-making process."[50]

As this continuing political behavior is observed, the five elements, or phases, of the political system emerge into view. While these will be discussed further in Chapter Three, in brief they are: (1) inputs (which may be demands or supports); (2) a conversion process (in which inputs are converted into outputs, usually by a legislature); (3) outputs, chiefly as laws and policies; and (4) a feedback loop by which the members of the society make further demands on, or offer continuing support for, the political system. The members of the society, that is, the folks who live within the purview of the political system, are a part of (5) the social environment of the system. Of course, the "environment" of the system can include its geographic surroundings, as well as its international environment. In practice, the axiom guides the attention of the political scientist to those components. Because observers know what to look at, i.e., "politics," they will soon see far more than what the axiom states, as a functioning political system unfolds before them.[51]

Political Life as Human Life

Throughout his discussion, Easton stated his axiom in slightly different variations, and also mentioned some qualifying nuances he intended but which are not always specified in his definition of politics. For example, he notes that out of all the forms of social activity some are "closely related to what we call political life."[52] Indeed, one key element of Easton's axiom is that it contemplates "life;" specifically, "the political aspects of life," or "the political side of life."[53] By "life," of course, he means human life. He observes, for instance, that "What we have in the concrete social world is a series of events in which human beings are involved."[54] He also wrote, "As a social system, a society is a special kind of human grouping the members of which continually interact with one another and in the process develop a sense of belonging together [or,] common consciousness."[55] He notes that "we are human beings who live in an organized society."[56] While this may seem too obvious to merit mentioning, as we will see, his stress on human life has important methodological and epistemological implications.[57]

The Axiom as a Rule of Relevance

Guided by his axiom, Easton writes that "Political life concerns all those varieties of activity that influence significantly the kind of authoritative policy adopted for a society and the way it is put into practice. We are said to be participating in political life when our activity relates in some way to the making and execution of policy for society."[58] For him, then, a phrase like *"relates in some way to* the making and execution of policy for society"* becomes a normative criteria, or rule, by which political scientists can make crucial research decisions. He writes, "If the object of [a field] theory is to identify all the important variables, some criteria are required to determine relevance or importance. … Without some guide to the investigator to indicate when a variable is politically relevant, social life would simply be an incoherent wilderness of activities."[59]

The rule, or norm, can give guidance as to what is to be included or excluded in a study, what is central, peripheral, or just unrelated to the subject matter. On the margins, however, there will be room for individual judgment, disagreement, and debate. As we see in the quote above, besides "relates in some way," Easton also uses the phrase "activity that influences significantly" policy and its implementation.[60] So it would seem that Easton meant to tighten up his rule to make only that which *significantly influences* policy relevant to the study of politics. However, Easton does not spell out what activities are a "significant" influence, nor how direct and determinative an influence should be to be relevant. Indeed, he then gives the rule broader scope when he states that it is political "whenever activity arise over the authoritative allocation of values, however *indirectly* this activity may be related to policy."[61] In line with this broader interpretation of the rule he published research on the subject of the political socialization of children.[62]

Intimacy and Method

As we have seen, at the time of writing *The Political System*, Easton regretted "the absence of a conceptual framework or systematic theory to give meaning, coherence, and direction to ongoing research."[63] He further regretted that political science then was unable to "provide the basis for the kind of understanding of their data that students of political life seek."[64] What kind of understanding is that? Easton was dissatisfied with what could be called the "dry data" approach of hyperfactual political science. Because "politics" involves an important dimension of human *life,* his view was that the true student of "political life" would want to feel some life connection to the subject. He referred to this connection as "intimacy," and understood this feeling as being an essential aspect of political science research.

He hoped that his axiom, and the framework implied by it, would not only help to guide and cultivate a "keen sense of where and how to look for the locus of power and its influence,"[65] but would awake in researchers "a deep awareness of the need to seek out *intimacy* with observed phenomena."[66] Easton thus anticipated the need for what would later become known as the repertoire of mixed methods advocated for, and practiced by, interpretive political science.

Writing in 1953, Easton noted that political science is currently behind the other social sciences in its use of the "repertoire of techniques for controlled observation, such as the varieties of highly developed forms of interview and objective participation, the correlation of data, experimentation, and the testing of theories."[67] Clearly, he expected that researchers would draw upon the wide variety of methods available in all the social sciences. For, as he understood, it is not the method but the axiom that defines the field of political science. He laments that in his day the use of mere fact gathering "techniques has had the secondary result of keeping the research student from intimate contact with his [or her] material."[68]

Easton rejected those more positivistic orientations that envision a mechanistic theory of human action as a series of learned, or programmed, reactions to stimuli. This robotic view eschews *empathy* and blinds itself to both the uniqueness of each political actor, and to the role of meaning and volition in behavior. He found unacceptable "the damaging effects of this lack of intimate knowledge about political activity on the products of research."[69] That "damage" is, of course, the lack of human understanding needed to solve some of the most pressing political problems of the day.[70]

Since Easton's axiom directs attention to the human element of politics, the question of how to obtain "intimate knowledge" of political actors arises in his approach, whereas such an inquiry is immaterial, if not inconceivable, in the positivistic approach dominant in his time (and ours). Also, in Easton's methodology, the researcher can approach the subject matter from different perspectives, such as putting the focus on the institutional "political process," or on "political behavior."[71] The former, more systemic meaning, "refers to the concrete system of intertwined activity which shapes authoritative policy."[72] But the latter, more intersubjective "behavioral" approach, focuses on "a particular aspect of data, the psychological."[73] When taking the behavioralist perspective as Easton understands it, political scientists "are studying the political process by looking at the relation to it of the motivations, personalities, or feelings of the participants as individual human beings."[74] This particular type of behavioral approach, what Easton meant by the term "behavioralism," can obtain the intimate knowledge that students of political life seek.

In Easton's behavioralism, then, for the political scientist to obtain intimate knowledge of the "attitudes … motivations and feelings of the human actor" [75] empathic interpretations of political behavior must be employed. Thus, Easton sees "a broad scope for direct field research … to make personal observations in the field according to acceptable standards for the collection of data." [76] What Easton adds to our understanding of political science knowledge, then, is that it includes a significant element of empathically knowing those feelings, meanings, and motivations experienced by actors *in relation to* the authoritative allocation of values for a society. Clearly, Easton's idea of political science knowledge includes far more than what the statisticians and mathematicians would include. While important, their brand of abstract knowledge is unable to achieve the kind of intimacy Easton envisions. In Chapter Three I will discuss further how this "intimate knowledge" is a core element of Easton's conception of political science knowledge.

The Axiom Compels Interpretive Methods

Easton's axiom not just implies, but compels the inclusion of qualitative/interpretive methods in political science. If political science is the study of behavior undertaken in relation to politics, then *the intentions* of the actor are determinative of the behavior's relevance. Whether an actor defines himself or herself as acting in a politically relevant way is a matter for the political scientist to determine through empathic observation, or interview, or some related technique. The behavior of a crowd at a football game can be similar to that of a crowd at a political rally. The meanings and intentions of the actors, less than their physical movements, determine which crowd is a fit subject for political science.

Political groups, therefore, are defined first by the political intentions of their members. Mere numbers of people make no sense unless their shared meanings are known. Thus, even large-N studies require an element of empathy. How is a potential voting block to be known, except by the understanding of the shared intentions and meanings that relate the individual persons to one another? What determines the relevance to political science as between a group of persons sitting in a living room for a Tupperware party, or a baby shower, and one gathered for a candidate fundraiser? It is their respective intentions and shared meanings. As Easton notes, observing behavior is not enough, the political scientist "must also be prepared to show what makes it political."[77] It is the intentions, and understanding intentions requires empathic interpretation.

Equilibrium Theory

Easton was quite insistent that the idea of "equilibrium theory," which became popular in his day, had no place in his understanding of the political system. In his view, the political system is a continuing process of human interactions undertaken in relation to the authoritative allocation of values for a society. For Easton, the word "process" means that the system does not seek equilibrium either as a goal or as a static state. A process is a continuing operation which, among other things, operates to preserve itself. But the persistence of the system is a continuing challenge, and the term "equilibrium" fails to convey the dynamics that every political system is involved in.

For example, Easton took exception to some of the basic assumptions in a political science textbook that was very influential among his contemporaries. In *The Process of Government*,[78] Arthur Bentley characterized political behavior in mechanistic terms, and as seeking equilibrium. Bentley assumes that individual political actors are automatons driven by their "interests" to form groups through which to pursue their political desires. This activity results in pressures that competing groups put upon one another. In the course of this process, each group anticipates "the response that a particular activity will stimulate [in competing groups] and then … acts accordingly."[79]

For instance, suppose an anti-abortion group puts pressure on Congress to pass a bill outlawing all abortions in the whole country, without exceptions even for rape, incest, or the mother's health. That will probably trigger a massive response from the pro-abortion side, which will likely pressure Congress to kill the bill. But if the bill is written to allow abortions during the first trimester of pregnancy, and during the second trimester where rape, incest, or the mother's health is at issue, then the opposition will likely not be strong enough to pressure Congress to prevent the bill from passing. Political groups, then, in Bentley's view, are entities which seek to maximize their gains by calculating the amount of pressure competing groups can muster in opposition. The political process is in "equilibrium" when a balance of power exists between competing groups, so that each group is maximizing its power in relation to all the other groups competing for government resources and favors.

While at first this may seem like a realistic depiction of politics, for Easton it is actually an unrealistic distortion of human political behavior. Easton rejects Bentley's mechanical analogy which casts the political process as "a complex reactive system that constantly tended towards a moment of balance or equilibrium."[80] He derisively calls this "a hydraulic theory of power."[81]

That theory tramples on the nuances of human behavior. Bentley's mechanism lacks isomorphism with the volitional and vital nature of political life. Political actors appear to have no inner volition, but are compulsively interest driven and reactive. Indeed, "Bentley specifically rejects [the] psychological approach in terms of feelings, attitudes, and [the] ideas of participants in political events. The actions of the groups must be interpreted, he holds, as responses to the pressures of other groups."[82] Easton finds it unacceptable that "Bentley would recognize, other than activity, no such variables as the personalities or the feelings of the participants."[83]

Bentley's theory is a reductionistic mutilation of the political process that actually blinds the political scientist to the human dimension of human political behavior. Political actors, whether individuals or groups, are not automatons which only act upon the calculations they make in the pursuit of their interests. Bentley's "objective" image of political actors as automatons is not compatible with the meaning Easton intends for his axiom. Easton's frequent references to "political life" as a form of "life," and to social interaction as human activity, show that he understood "life" as implying complex, animate, sentient, intelligent organisms, not colliding particles or pool balls in motion. Easton especially takes exception to Bentley's exclusion of the meaning making minds of actors and the reduction of human groups to robotically moving about according to their strategic calculations. Easton remarks that Bentley's dehumanizing theory would "keep the motivations of the actors constant and thereby delete [their humanity] from the situation."[84] Thus Bentley's stimulus-response model is incompatible with Easton's interpretive humanism.

Alternatively, Easton favors the approach of sociologist Robert K. Merton, whose idea of "Normative Science" we discussed in the Introduction. For understanding and explaining human action, Merton uses the theory of "the definition of the situation." This approach is more *realistic* in that it assumes the intelligence, creativity, and therefore "the indeterminacy of [human] behavior."[85] In this view, political actors tend to act in accord with the way they understand, or define, the political meaning of a situation. "No two individuals will define a situation and react to it in exactly the same way. The same facts may be so interpreted by two different persons as to lead to totally divergent decisions and actions."[86] One of the challenges of political scientists, then, is to accurately and empathically interpret the *reasons* that people have for engaging in political behavior.

The philosopher of science, and contemporary of Easton, Michael Polanyi has observed, "To represent [persons] as insentient is empirically false, but to regard them as thoughtful automata is logical nonsense."[87] Easton criticized Bentley, and his ilk, on both grounds.[88]

Reasons as Causes

Easton's axiom based theory of the political system, also stands as a complete alternative to the positivistic framework, which has no rule for determining what is the relative subject matter of political science. And, as we have seen, Easton rejects the mechanical and deterministic theory of human behavior so widely ascribed to by positivists. Instead, "politics" is envisioned as the volitional behavior of persons and groups of persons who are intentionally engaged in matters related to the authoritative allocation of values for society.[89]

Easton's assumption that humans create the meanings by which they define the political situations they are in, and then act upon those meanings, explodes the old positivistic notion of personally detached "objective" observations of behavior, and compels the position of *personally involved* empathic observation and interpretation. Under Easton's principles, then, the explanation of behavior necessarily entails an exposition of the observer's understanding of the *reasons* the actors had for their behavior. In some cases, groups and individuals may not fully understand their own motivations, or even misrepresent them. The political scientist can empathically observe and then clarify these motivations.

With the principle that reasons can be the causes of behavior, the idea of causation remains, but the mechanistic tendency is factored out by the axiom's implication of people as volitional, creative, intelligent, meaning making sentient beings. This softer theory of causation recognizes that for any volitional action, it could have been otherwise. In addition, the hope for a way to verify or refute hypotheses, in the manner of laboratory physics, must give way to a requirement more like the intersubjective confirmation or criticism of findings by peers. No one can, for instance, replicate in a laboratory a participant observer's experience and observations for later analysis. But peers can criticize the methods and logic used, and based on their own experience and personal judgment, credit contributions to knowledge. In this sense, then, the conduct of Easton's interpretive behavioralism would be, as Merton said of science, a community project, working within a shared interpretive framework, and drawing from a plurality of methods.[90]

Conclusion: Easton's Two Meanings of the "Political System"

Easton notes that he uses the concept of the political system "in two different but related senses."[91] One usage is in reference to the actual "empirical behavior which we observe and characterize as political life [and that] as students of politics, we wish to understand and explain. We can speak of this phenomenal reality as the empirical or behaving system."[92] This behavioral political system is political life in action, struggling for survival, or persistence, in its environment.

Easton writes that his other usage of the term is in reference to the symbolic construct, theoretical framework, or definition of "the political system" as patterns of interaction undertaken in relation to the authoritative allocation of values for a society. This conceptual political system "corresponds to the behaving system which it is designed to explain."[93] In other words, the distinction he is making is between the political system both as an interpretive framework, and as the subject matter to which the framework refers – the actual behavior which constitutes a political system. Easton insists that it "is of the utmost importance to keep these two kinds of systems distinct."[94]

In the next chapter, Chapter Two, I will offer an evidence-based hypothesis for the origins of the first pattern of actual "political behavior." That pattern developed over thousands of years of pre-human evolution. We will see how the hominids out of whom Homo sapiens evolved had set the stage for the human behavior that constitutes a political system.

In Chapter Three I will show how Easton's *theoretical* statement of the political system, its definition, can serve two *normative* purposes. The first is as a guide to political science research. The second normative use for the definition of the political system is as a standard for assessing how well a particular behavioral political system is operating.

Chapter Four will illustrate the application of this operational standard to the assessment of how well the political system of China is operating. That Chapter will follow the logic of assessment. Chapter Five will discuss what sorts of organizational changes in the political science profession can be made to accommodate the adoption of Normative Political Science as its organizational paradigm.

ENDNOTES

[12.] Gunnell 2013, 198.

[13.] Ibid..

[14.] Ibid.

[15.] Ibid., 205.

[16.] I appreciate the encouragement Professor Gunnell has given me in our private communications.

[17] There are many instances supporting Gunnell's observation that *The Political System* has become "a prisoner of … its interpretive history." For example, in a survey of approaches to the study of politics, Mark Bevir classifies Easton as a "behaviouralists," and behavioralism as an "expression of the turn toward positivism." Bevir then defines the "positivist concept of science" as seeking "universal, deductive, predictive, and verifiable theory." Easton is thus labeled in a way that completely obscures the uniqueness of his axiom centered political theory, which, as we will show, is actually quite distinct from positivism. See Bevir 2006, quote at page 18 in online version.

[18.] Easton 1953, 1971, 52.

[19.] Easton 1953, 1971, 65.

[20.] Easton 1953, 1971, 96.

[21.] Easton 1953, 1971, 6.

[22.] See *The Political System*, Chapter Three, pp 64-89. Throughout the book he distinguished this understanding from the narrow positivistic sense of 19th century mechanics, as we discuss in this chapter. He also distinguishes between pure science (seeking knowledge in itself), and applied science (knowledge used to support recommendations for political reform). See ibid, pages 87-89.

[23.] Easton 1953, 1971, 92.

[24.] Easton 1953, 1971, 93, 98.

[25.] Easton 1953, 1971, 47. The phrase "born free but is everywhere in chains" is borrowed from Rousseau's *Social Contract.*

[26.] Easton 1953, 1971, 66. Easton sees his views as part of the "modern psychology of perception," and mocks the "pure empiricist tradition" of "objective observation" as a theory of an "immaculate perception." In "Easton Responds to Classical Critics," online at https://isistatic.org/journal-archive/pr/03_01/easton.pdf, ND (but early 1970s), page 278f. This places him even further from positivistic notions of "scientific objectivity."

[27.] Easton 1953, 1971, 53.

[28.] Easton 1953, 1971, 53.

[29.] Easton 1953, 1971, 53. Cf. Hawkesworth's discussion of "presupposition theory," in Yanow et al 2014, 27-49.

30. Easton 1953, 1971, 100.

31. Easton 1953, 1971, 147.

32. Easton 1953, 1971, 99.

33. Easton 1953, 1971, 103.

34. Easton 1953, 1971, 104.

35. Easton 1953, 1971, 104.

36. Easton 1953, 1971, 96.

37. Easton 1953, 1971, 99.

38. Easton 1953, 1971, 144, n12. Easton's phrases concerning "the intrinsic logic" of each field, and field's having "a rationale of their own" along with his references to the "intuition" and "feel" that founding figures had for their fields, refer to pre-conceptual understandings that have yet to be brought up to the level of a clearly defined axiom.

The intellectual interests and aptitudes of such pioneering researchers discussed by Easton are close to Michael Polanyi's conception of "Intellectual passions." See Polanyi 1958.

39. Easton 1953, 1971, 127.

40. Easton 1953, 1971, 127.

41. Easton 1953, 1971, 54.

42. Easton 1953, 1971, 59.

43. Easton 1953, 1971, 60.

44. Cf. Easton 1953, 1971, 128, 129 passim. My understanding of the part an axiom can play in a system of thought comes from the philosopher of science, Robert S. Hartman. See Hartman 1967.

45. Easton 1953, 1971, 128.

46. Easton's axiom is both the core and the wellspring of his systematic theory. Like corrective eye lenses, it focuses and clarifies one's vision of the scope and methods for political science. Like a metaphor, the axiom implicates, but does not describe, the entire field of political science, which lies waiting for future discoveries. Originating as Easton's own creative construct, it is derived from a thorough study of the then existing literature. He understood that the axiom is not itself an empirically verifiable hypothesis. He wrote, "if political theory as an area of research should measure up to its tasks [of illuminating the field, such a] systematic theory, while empirically relevant, would nonetheless not necessarily be readily reducible to verifiable propositions." Easton 1953, 1971, 317. And, a "highly general theory," such as his, may be "too abstract for immediate application to the facts." Easton 1953, 1971, 314ff. Easton advised that "at a high level of abstraction," such as his axiom, "theory needs to be free to develop unhampered by excessive worries of verification." Easton 1953, 1971, 315. This statement alone greatly distinguishes Easton from positivism,

which, as we will discuss further below, insists that theories be verifiable.

[47.] As to how the pattern of life constituting the first political system emerged in human evolution, see Chapter Two herein.

[48.] Easton 1953, 1971, 97.

[49.] Easton 1953, 1971, 78.

[50.] Easton 1953, 1971, 129.

[51.] Some readers of *The Political System* might find it ironic that given its title, Easton does not elaborate specifically on the components of his theory of the political system in that book. Instead, he carries out an extended presentation of that theory in two succeeding works, *A Framework for Political Analysis*, Easton 1965a. And *A Systems Analysis of Political Life*. Easton 1965b. Those works, rich in insights and guidance for the conduct of political science, and Easton's "input/output" theory, will be discussed in Chapter Three. For Easton to elaborate on the elements of the theory of the political system would have been a distraction from his central aim of *The Political System,* which is to introduce his axiom, and to show the need for a systematic political theory and the lack thereof in political science. That is why he notes that the "merest hint of a theory [of the political system] that does emerge is incidental here to the main purpose." Easton 1953, 1971, page 5. But because he understood that observing political life through the lens of the axiom culminates in a view of the political system, a book introducing the axiom and explaining the need for it is aptly titled *The Political System* – the ultimate implication of the axiom. In other words, the creative conception of the axiom both enabled and led to the construction of the theory of the political system.

[52.] Easton 1953, 1971, 97.

[53.] Easton 1953, 1971, 96, 126.

[54.] Easton 1953, 1971, 53.

[55.] Easton 1953, 1971, 135.

[56.] Ibid, page Easton 1953, 1971, 103.

[57.] As to why chimpanzee "politics" do not rise to the level of a political system, see Kelleher, "Can Chimpanzee Politics Constitute a Political System?"

[58.] Easton 1953, 1971, 128.

[59.] Easton 1953, 1971, 98.

[60.] Easton 1953, 1971, 128.

[61.] Easton 1953, 1971, 192, emp. ad.

[62.] See Easton and Dennis 1969, 1967.

[63.] Easton 1953, 1971, 52.

[64.] Easton 1953, 1971, 51.

[65.] Easton 1953, 1971, 52.

[66.] Easton 1953, 1971, 52, emp. ad.

[67] Easton 1953, 1971, 49.

[68] Easton 1953, 1971, 49.

[69] Easton 1953, 1971, 49.

[70] Easton 1953, 1971, 49.

[71] Easton 1953, 1971, 203.

[72] Easton 1953, 1971, 204-205.

[73] Easton 1953, 1971, 205.

[74] Easton 1953, 1971, 205.

[75] Easton 1953, 1971, 201.

[76] Easton 1953, 1971, 49.

[77] Easton 1953, 1971, 192.

[78] *The Process of Government*, by Arthur Bentley (1908, 1949) University of Chicago Press. Easton cites David Truman's *The Governmental Process*, 1951, as having a "heavy dependence on Bentley." Ibid., 176, note 6.

[79] Easton, *The Political System*, id., p178

[80] Ibid., 271.

[81] Ibid., 177.

[82] Ibid., 178.

[83] Ibid., 179.

[84] Ibid., 180.

[85] Easton 1953, 1971, pages 25-31. Easton and Merton were contemporaries who both earned degrees at Harvard, and both seem to have been influenced by the social psychologist George Herbert Mead whose work was gaining in popularity when they were students. Indeed, Gunnell relates that as an undergrad Easton started out in political science, but "attempted to transfer to sociology at the end of his sophomore year, [however] university rules did not allow the change." Gunnell supra at page 192.

[86] Ibid., 200-201; cf. pp26-31, and p178f.

[87] Polanyi 1958, page 339. The absence of references to both Polanyi and Hartman in *The Political System* and later works suggests that Easton had not been familiar with the work of either philosopher.

[88] Although Easton criticized "equilibrium theory" extensively to be sure that his political theory was not associated with that very notion, he is often lumped in with it. For example, in his history of the Caucus for a New Political Science, Clyde Barrow states that the "central focus" of Easton's approach is "to understand how 'decision-making' (i.e., authoritative allocations of values) facilitate the *equilibrium* of the overall social system," at page 217 (emp. ad.). Barrow 2008, pages 216-217. Another instance of conflating Easton with other writers under the rubrics "behavioral political science" and "functionalism" is by Mary Hawkesworth. She writes that for Easton, as for these schools of thought,

the political system is seen as functioning "so as to maintain homeostatic equilibrium." See Hawkesworth, "Contending Conceptions of Science and Politics," page 46, in Yanow 2014. But, for Easton, nothing could be further from the truth. See Kelleher WPSA paper 2017.

[89.] Understanding the behavior as volitional adds to the challenge of explaining how a political system is able to persist. Every day, large numbers of individuals and groups act in ways that preserve their political system, although at any time they could choose to do otherwise, as they do in revolutions.

[90.] See Polanyi 1946, 1958. An activist in the paradigm politics of his day, and apparently in an effort to maintain his alliance with his contemporary "behavioralists," Easton introduced what he called the "behavioralist credo" in *A Framework for Political Analysis.* Easton 1965a, page 7. This is a list of eight Mertonian-like "norms" which he says binds the behavioralists together. He immediately follows this "Credo" with a set of equivocations that will allow him to disregard any constraints they might place on his own approach: "No single way of characterizing [these postulates] is satisfactory to everyone." Easton 1965a, page 6. He further acknowledged that even among behavioralists there would surely be "major differences," especially "about the relative prominence of one or another of the [eight] articles." Easton 1965a, page 9. Politically shrewd as this tactic may or may not be, as a consequence of so closely allying himself with the supposed "behavioralist movement," Easton diminishes the uniqueness of his own systematic political theory and invites others to do the same. In this sense, then, Easton shares in the responsibility for the current situation in which, as Gunnell has observed, *The Political System* has become "a prisoner of ... its interpretive history." Gunnell 2013, 198.

[91.] Easton, A Framework, 1965, p. 26

[92.] Ibid.

[93.] Ibid.

[94.] Ibid.

Chapter Two:

The Origins of Human Political Behavior in Early Hominid Food Sharing

Introduction[1]

The idea of the political system is well established in political science. In this essay I will rely on the time-honored definition given by former American Political Science Association president, David Easton.[2] Easton's theory is that, out of all the behavior of people in a society, particular patterns of social interactions can be observed and identified as "political behavior." Individual and group activity becomes "political" when it is undertaken in relation to "the authoritative allocation of values for a society." In short, "politics," in Easton's interpretive framework, is the decision making process for establishing and enforcing public policy. Unlike Aristotle, the "father of political science," Easton's focus is not on the form of government a society has, such as democracy, oligarchy, or monarchy, but on the *actual behavior* of groups and individuals. That behavior is what forms the system.

For Easton, the dynamic process of political behavior inevitably follows a systematic pattern. No matter what society one is observing, whether high-tech, low-tech, north, south, east, or west, "political behavior" produces the pattern of the political system. That is, there are 1) "inputs," in the form of demands for particular policies, or member support or disapproval for the governing regime as shown, for instance in polling or letter writing. There are 2) "conversions," or the government's policy making process, whether in response to inputs or on its own initiative. 3) "outputs," or the actual policies, legislation, and implementation that comes out of the conversion process; and, 4) "feedback," negative or positive, from the members of the political system, whether the public or interested elites. This self-reflective dynamic takes place in 5) an "environment," which includes natural and cultural conditions.

Political behavior, producing the pattern of the political system, can be seen taking place right now, all over the world. Not only are people in China, Russia, and the United States busily creating their political systems, but so are all the 193 member nations of the United Nations.[3] Indeed, folks in such societies as the Maasai tribe in east central Africa, the Iroquois Confederacy in North America, and the Yanomami in the northern Amazon, are doing likewise.[4]

Of course, all this political behavior, happening right now, did not just "pop" into existence. Because society is an event that has emerged in the course of evolution, political behavior, too, emerged at some point in evolution. My quest, in this essay, will be to try and find the very first pattern of political behavior in the long stretch of evolution. That is, the first patterns of behavior to rise to the level of a "political system" – the common ancestor which all contemporary political systems replicate. We will see that to understand the origins of the first political system, we must venture into the far distant past of human ancestry, way beyond the invention of written records over 5000 years ago. Indeed, we will go well past the time when Homo sapiens emerged in evolution, roughly two hundred thousand years ago[5] and examine the ways our pre-human, hominid, ancestors lived.

While this project is intended to shed new light on one of the core concepts in contemporary political science, the political system, I will draw upon the knowledge, and empathic wisdom, of such other sciences as archaeology, paleoanthropology, animal breeding, population genetics, and prehistory.

Glynn Isaac's Food Sharing Model

One area of the world intensively studied by scientists seeking to learn how pre-humans lived is that section of the Great Rift Valley running through eastern Africa. For our purposes, by far the most significant of the reported research is that by the late Harvard archaeologist, Glynn Isaac (1978). He, along with Richard Leakey (1979), son of famed paleontologists Mary and Louis Leakey (1971), excavated several sites in the Koobi Fora region on the northeastern shore of Lake Turkana, Kenya. As Mary and Louis Leakey had earlier found in the Olduvai Gorge area of Tanzania, the Koobi Fora sites were rich in ancient pre-human remains, and hints about their behavior. (1978, 94). Isaac wrote of the discoveries he and his research team had made, not only to report the facts, but to interpret them. His most provocative thesis, and crucial to our concerns, is his "food sharing model" of how early pre-human hominids lived in these several scattered sites of east Africa. The time frame for these sites was generally from 2.5 to 1.5mya ("million years ago"). Isaac sees the sites as indicating a critical moment in the evolution of human behavior. And, as I will argue, this "food sharing" moment was also key to the emergence of the first political system.

As in Olduvai Gorge, different types of sites were found at Koobi Fora. Some had only stone tools. Some had stone tools and the bones of "a single large animal" (1978, 95f). Others had stone tools and the bones of "several different animal species" (1978, 95). The first type of site may have been a kind of "factory," where hominids gathered simply to make stone tools, which they did by smashing one rock against another (1978, 99). The second type of site may have been one which stone tools were brought to for the purpose of cutting up the carcass of an animal too large to be moved elsewhere. For instance, one site had stone tools, but only the bones of a hippopotamus (1978, 96). The third type of site has both stone tools and the bones from a variety of animals, such as the leg bones of antelopes, and bones from the whole carcasses of smaller wild life.

Isaac bases his food sharing model on these eastern African discoveries.   He imaginatively interprets the implications of these excavations for the probable behavior of the hominids that created the sites. For his food sharing model, the evidence of stone tools associated with a variety of animal bones suggests that hominids repeatedly, and I would add, intentionally, brought their stone tools and meat bearing animal carcasses and body parts to a mutually agreed upon place for the purpose of cutting up the meat and sharing it with one another. Isaac refers to such places as "home bases." If true, this behavior suggests, among other things, a significant degree of planning depth and communication. While there may have been other types, or breeds, of hominid living in eastern Africa during this period, Isaac proposes that the food sharing ones "were directly ancestral to modern man" (1978, 96).

Isaac's image of hominid behavior has numerous implications, and raises many questions, some of which Isaac addresses. For example, did these pre-human hominids obtain their meat by hunting, or scavenging? Did they have a division of labor? If so, how was it, and other social relations, organized and maintained? What language skills did they have?

Meat Eating Hunters

The site with the hippopotamus bones raises a contentious issue. That is whether the hominids hunted down and killed the animal, or "came upon it dead" (1978, 96-97). Isaac finds the evidence unclear either way. However, he does not see these hominids as the ferocious hunters of popular mythology. "Given the low level of stone technology in evidence. I am inclined to suspect scavenging rather than hunting" (1978, 97, cf. 102). Indeed, with little more than rocks and clubs in hand, the hominids of this period, which were under five feet tall, would have had to come in so close to a large animal, like a huge hippo, that they would have run a high risk of being bitten and stomped to death, while inflicting only minor injuries on the beast. Hence, "it seems less reasonable to assume that protohumans, armed primitively if at all, would be particularly effective hunters" (1978, 102). They may have hunted, or trapped, smaller animals, around the size of a small pig, "but the flesh of larger animals was probably available only through scavenging" (1978, 104. For a recent study in agreement see O'Connell et al. 2002).

Articulating the Food Sharing Model

Isaac notes that "we know for a fact that somewhere along the line in the evolution of human behavior two patterns became established: food-sharing and a division of labor" (1978, 100). However, Isaac is less certain about what other forms of behavior belong in his food sharing model. He understood that his food sharing model is not a fully articulated paradigm of hominid behavior, and he expected succeeding researchers to work on filling out the model. While there were still many unknowns for him, he suggests that it might be helpful to consider the behavior of contemporary apes, especially the chimpanzee, and that of "hunter-gatherer" groups still living in Africa (1978, 93). Perhaps these comparisons can serve as a useful aid in imagining what sorts of behavior went into the making of the sites excavated in eastern Africa.

Isaac's Comparisons

First among Isaac's comparisons is the obvious fact that humans are bipedal, and can carry things even as they walk long distances. Hunter-gatherers use containers, such as trays, baskets, and bags, to increase the amounts of items they can carry. Upright walking and containers facilitate food sharing. Chimps, in contrast, are primarily knuckle walkers, and do not use devices for carrying. Carrying things by hand any substantial distance is too difficult for them as knuckle walkers (1978, 90).

Chimpanzee Food Sharing

From the point of view of the food sharing model, a very significant distinction between primate and hunter-gatherer behavior becomes apparent. That is, the individual primate is primarily a self-feeding forager. With few exceptions, such as maternal behavior, while feeding and moving about as a group, the mature individual primate is responsible for his or her food acquisition. In contrast, for most hunter-gatherers, "the acquisition of food is a corporate responsibility" (1978, 92). Unlike primates, hunter-gatherers commonly share food within their group as a central part of their "primary subsistence adaptation" (1978, 90, 92). "Food is exchanged between adults, and it is shared between adults and juveniles" (1978, 92).

While hunter-gatherers share all types of food, "Vegetable foods, which are the great apes' principal diet, are not shared and are almost invariably consumed by each individual on the spot." (1978, 93). Also, like other primates, chimps only "occasionally feed on meat." When a male hunts down a monkey, other chimps become excited and beg for a portion. Isaac calls this "scrounging." The male might parcel out pieces, but generally does this strategically. He either rewards allied males or buys favor with females. As Isaac comments, this behavior "falls far short of active sharing" (1978, 92).[6] Thus, because food sharing is quite marginal for primate survival, perhaps the behavior of hunter-gatherers is more indicative of how the food sharing hominids lived.[7]

Projection

Isaac does not claim that any of the examples of our hunter-gatherer cohorts was the way the food sharing hominids actually behaved. As he noted, "one must strongly resist the temptation to project too much of ourselves into the past." After all, "the hominid life systems of two million years ago have no living counterparts" (1978, 104). Instead, the items on his lists of behaviors are intended to be hypotheses made "explicit so that [they] can be tested and revised" (1978, 108, cf. 101f).

Isaac in a Larger Context

Having sketched out Isaac's model for the hominid way of life, I will discuss some of the reactions to it by succeeding scientists. As we will see, some of them doubt the model's efficacy, while others offer more constructive criticisms and insights both to clarify it and to amplify it. This discussion will show how and why Isaac's food sharing model is the foundation for our explanation of the emergence of the first political system.

But first I will address some preliminary questions about hominid life prior to the period of Isaac's model. For instance, how did hominids live *before* at least some of them became food sharers? Was it like their primate cousins, as self-feeding foragers? If so, how and why did the hominids of Isaac's model become food sharers? How was the transition to the food sharing way of life accomplished?

The Split

Isaac recognizes that the story of how food sharing came about for the hominids he studied begins with the initial divergence from a common ancestor to both the chimpanzee lineage and the hominid lineage. (1978, 94). He points out that experts disagree as to the exact time frame in which this speciation event took place. Besides differences of professional opinion, different methods for estimating the time frame can lead to vastly different numbers. Isaac notes that it "is not yet established beyond doubt whether the divergence occurred a mere five to six million years ago, as [some scientists] argue on biochemical grounds, or 15 to 20 million years ago, as many paleontologists believe on the grounds of fossil evidence." (1978, 93).

But since Isaac made that observation, in the early 1970s, more of a consensus has developed among the scientists who have studied the matter. While far from having an exact measure, the weight of opinion among paleoanthropologists, geneticists, and other scientists is that this split, or divergence, falls between five and seven million years ago. [8]

One reason for this broad spread of time from the last common ancestor to the appearance of the hominid species is that the speciation process generally does not happen overnight. In this case, the process likely took place gradually, over millions of years, and it was far from a uniform progression.[9] Paleontologists have discovered the bones of many types of hominids. These findings form a spotty mosaic of new variants appearing here and there, rather than a clear course of development towards a particular end. The hominid type that Isaac depicts in his food sharing model is but one piece of that mosaic.

Let us suppose, then, that the split in the course of evolution between chimps and hominids began roughly 6mya. Suppose we also agree with Isaac that by 2mya food sharing was "already part of a novel adaptive strategy" for at least one group of hominids (1978, 94). One challenge for interpretation is, then, to try to explain what likely happened in the four million years between Point A (when the split began) and Point B (when food sharing hominids emerged). In the following paragraphs, I will take on that challenge.

Speciation and Sexual Selection

Different forms of life generally develop out of a process of speciation. Typically, in an animal species, for instance, some members of a group within a species become geographically separated from their breeding community. The members of the separated group become reproductively isolated from their kind. Of course, members of the separated group continue inter-breeding. Genetic mutations occur in all populations, and when this happens in an isolated group, a mutation can become a characteristic of the group.

Perhaps a mutation gives some adaptive advantage to the members of the group. For example, the giraffe's long neck enables it to reach nutritious leaves and fruits high in the trees, as well as see potential predators in the grass and bushes. Members of the species with shorter necks had less access to the nutritious food, and were less able to see approaching predators. As shorter neck individuals were eliminated, the former mutation for growing a long neck became a fixed characteristic in the species by a process of natural selection.

But a genetic mutation can also become fixed in the genome of a species by another route; that is, sexual selection. Darwin's favorite example of this process is the multi-colored, wonderfully patterned tail feathers of the peacock (or male pea) (1871, 126f). Suppose a group of ground feeding fowls had become reproductively isolated from its fellows. Among them a mutation for colored feathers in the tail of a male fowl appeared at random, and some of the females felt especially attracted to him as a lover. Some of the male offspring of his mating partners would have inherited the gene for colored feathers in their tails, and some females would have inherited the propensity to find such males irresistible. An upward spiral began, and eventually the current patterning became fixed in the genome of the species (Darwin 1871, Fisher 1930).

Last Common Ancestor

There are no fossil specimens of the last common ancestor to the chimpanzees and the hominids. But scientists seem to generally agree it was a gibbon-like creature. While some members of the species may have lived in Eurasia, others lived in east Africa. Indeed, the consensus of opinion is that the split took place in the Great Rift Valley, in eastern Africa. Since all primates, including chimpanzees, live as self-feeding foragers, it is likely that prior to the split this is how our last common ancestor was adapted to its environment (Isaac 1978). The creature probably preferred to dwell and forage in trees, with occasional forays on to *terra firma*. It was likely able to stand upright on tree limbs and on the ground. But it probably lacked the vertical backbone needed for regular upright walking. Perhaps it was around two feet tall, weighing up to 25 pounds (Nengo 2017).

Becoming reproductively isolated from this common stock, ancestors to the chimps began their trajectory of evolution, and ancestors to the hominids went their way. Both lineages grew physically, and both adapted to more ground living than their common ancestor. But the chimps have remained relatively attached to the trees, while the hominids became wholly ground dwellers. As Isaac noted, the chimps evolved up to the level of knuckle walking on the ground, while hominids developed skeletal structures adapted to exclusive upright walking. Along the way, individual hominids began sharing food more often than their primate relatives. One question left unanswered by Isaac is as to how this food sharing behavior could have begun?

The Start of Food Sharing

One way food sharing could have begun is that within at least one group of hominids a genetic mutation for a food sharing propensity began to appear. Because of Isaac's work, we know where this mutation leads. Isaac wondered how natural selection could have favored the development of this hominid characteristic. And he admits this "puzzle" stymied him (1978, 93-94). Perhaps he was stuck because he was asking the wrong question, or looking in the wrong places. He did not consider that food sharing was clearly not necessary for the survival of the hominid species. Those creatures could have gone on for as long as the chimps, and other primates, have, living as self-feeding foragers. So, contrary to Isaac's presupposition, the food sharing characteristic is not likely the result of natural selection. Most likely, the genetic basis for the food sharing propensity became fixed in this hominid's genome by sexual selection.

Because some hominids became food sharers, it is likely that a genetic based mating preference for individuals who shared food developed among the ancestors of those hominids. As we have seen, female peas probably developed a sexual preference for peacocks with beautiful plumage. However, Darwin's example of the peacocks assumes a male genetic lead, and a responsive attraction developing in the females. But the implication of a male initiator, and a relatively passive female response, is not a necessary, nor a proven, scientific principle. Sexual selection can entail a complex mix of motivations, as it fixes a characteristic in the genome of a species. An individual, whether male or female, could have both a propensity for food sharing, and a sexual attraction to those other hominids who display it, without one always being the initiator and the other always the responder.

Imagine a band of hominids self-feeding as they roam about their foraging range. A female finds a grub with a delightful flavor. She's never had one like this before. She picks up another one and offers it to a male acquaintance from her group, who happens to be foraging near her. Members of groups share life together. Her gesture is simply a continuation of that process, an expression of comradery. She need not have any self-interested ulterior motive, or scheme. Perhaps without words, she just gestures that he try it, simply because as a fellow creature he might like it, too.

Sharing this dining pleasure adds to the quality of their common bond as members of the same band. Also, generally, to share food requires physical proximity. Add all this together, and the next step is highly likely. The genetic proclivities entailed in this scenario are those for offering to share food, those for the receptivity to such an offer, and the mysterious complex of genetic codes resulting in sexual attraction.

Variations on this "girl meets boy" story would have had to have been repeated many times, over perhaps scores of generations, as a necessary step towards the end result that Isaac discusses. Gradually, these hominids bred themselves into creatures with a propensity for food sharing. As the process unfolded, there likely would have been interbreeding bands of hominids who, of necessity, continued to live primarily as self-feeding foragers, but also increasingly sharing food, because their inner desire to share food was in a genetic spiral due to their sexual preferences.

As their desire to share food increased, so would their alertness for opportunities to do so. As creatures who live by self-feeding while they forage, sharing opportunities are limited by the necessity to sit and chew the foods each feeds himself or herself. Chewing some raw foods can be more time consuming than chewing soft foods, or cooked foods. Since they did not have cooking, as yet, time spent chewing one's own food would cut down the time available for sharing, even if they wanted to share more. Food sharing has another practical limit within the forager social organization. Chaos would ensue if each forager always fed another, rather than himself or herself. So food sharing would have to be an incidental activity within the self-feeding way of life. To become exclusively food sharing would require transitioning to another form of social organization.

An Emergent Culture

As we all know, along their evolutionary way, hominids invented stone tools. Among other things, some stone tools could be used for preparing raw food to make it easier to chew. Tough tubers dug from the ground could be sliced, and the pieces pounded to soften them. Some hominids likely saw this as an opportunity for sharing. With tools, one band member could slice and pound turnips, while other members brought in some berries and insects, perhaps on bark trays. Such events were probably intermittent prior to becoming socially organized for the food sharing way of life. This occasional sharing is how a nascent division of labor, to facilitate food sharing, likely emerged in the hominid cultures that were taking shape along the Great Rift Valley in eastern Africa.

Mating preferences could have intensified this cultural trend. Selfish, non-cooperators may have been considered less desirable by both sexes. One tension involved in this transition is that self-feeding is *ipso facto* a selfish act, and it requires almost no cooperation. So the transition to a more cooperative culture would probably have involved considerable frustration and some conflict. Those with the stronger desire for cooperation so as to share food likely formed their own bands to minimize conflicts. Either they were driven out by the more selfish creatures, or they formed norms of their own, and banished the violators.

Hominid Social Organization

Isaac speculates that just as primates, as well as hunter-gatherers, pay much attention to social relations and hierarchies, so too the hominids of Koobi Fora and Olduvai Gorge were surely concerned with "the fine adjustment of social relations," particularly in the allocation of labor tasks and shares of food (1978, 106). Isaac admits, however, that in his day, little or nothing was actually known about the social organization, much less the politics, of the hominids who achieved the level of cooperative civilization displayed by the sites he and others have examined. As we will see, succeeding scientists would find evidence and construct theories to further explain what sort of social organization and politics were required to establish the food sharing society indicated by the evidence that Isaac, and others, had found.

Critiques of Isaac

In the field of hominid studies, Isaac's thesis that early hominids eventually transitioned from a self-feeding foraging way of life to a food sharing way of life is generally not in dispute. However, some of the concepts in his food sharing model have been critically examined by subsequent experts. His concept of the "home base," for instance, has drawn quite a bit of attention.

The archaeologist, Lewis Binford (1981, 2014), was strongly skeptical about Isaac's theories of hominid behavior. For Binford, the interpretations of the associations of bones and stones proposed by Isaac, the Leakeys, and others, were accepted too uncritically. He doubted that any inferences about hominid behavior were warranted by the sites, except that hominids were probably there, but only as scavengers for morsels of uneaten meat and the marrow in bones left by animals (2014, 282, 296).

In his view, Isaac's inferences about "home bases" improperly suggests long occupancy in places that may actually be only aggregates of refuse left behind, mostly by animals, over very long periods of time (2014, 296.) He suspects that notions about hominids "carrying food home" to share with their families are "wildly inaccurate," mere "myth making," and "just-so stories" (2014, 282, 251, 291). Binford makes fun of Isaac's model by presenting an exaggerated caricature of it as "a kind of middle class genteel protohuman who shared his food, took care of his family, and was on his way to being emotionally and intellectually human" (2014, 295f). Incidentally, Binford also rejects Robert Ardrey's widely read "fanciful" theory of early hominids as "killer apes." On this point, Binford agrees with Isaac that a careful scrutiny of the accepted evidence shows that our distant hominid ancestors in Africa probably did little or no hunting. For Binford, hunting as a regular practice likely began only after the bow and arrow made it safer to do so (2014, 296).

In line with the methods of positivistic natural science, Binford recoils from taking any but the most cautious steps of inference that would go beyond describing what is visible to the eye of the excavator in hominid studies. For example, "bone 21 was found lying six inches from stone 43," etc. Presumably, Binford's method would exclude empathic interpretations of hominid feelings and intentions. He does acknowledge that it is proper to ask what generated the conditions observed and described, but students of hominid life must "employ a reliable methodology for giving meanings to these facts as a way of gaining some idea if the conjectured past is anything like that past as in fact it occurred" (2014, 250).[10] Binford's critiques had the fortunate effect of prompting other experts in the field to take a closer look at Isaac's concepts.

Potts on Home Bases

As we have seen, Isaac offered his interpretations of the sites at Koobi Fora and Olduvai Gorge as hypotheses which he invited other scholars of the subject matter to test. Indeed, just a few years later, one such scholar, Richard Potts (1984), took up that task. After scrutinizing the evidence acquired by the excavators of these sites, Potts challenged some of the elements of Isaac's food sharing model.[11] In particular, like Binford, Potts argued that the characterization of these sites as "home bases" was unjustified. But Potts aimed to improve the model, not to reject it.

While Potts agreed with Isaac that observations of contemporary hunter-gatherer life could have some heuristic value for interpreting hominid behavior, he was stricter than Isaac in his insistence that neither the behavior of contemporary hunter-gatherers nor that of contemporary primates serves well as "a modern analogue" for explaining the activities of those early hominids (Potts 1984, 347, 339f; 1988, 8). Because times change, interpretation "requires an open mind to *uniqueness* in the activity of early hominids" (1984, 347 italics added). In his view, unlike Binford, the evidence does show that "hominids played an important role in the formation" of at least some of the sites under study (1984, 343). The problem, then, is to try to understand what kind of activities went on at these sites (1984, 343). If the early hominids were not making "home bases," then what were they doing? (1984, 342-343).

The popular image of the contemporary hunter-gatherer home base generally entails an encampment, with huts, campfires, and inhabitants sharing food and taking care of their young, elderly, etc. Potts notes while this picture is not always accurate, and rarely an analogue to early hominid life, it entails "two important aspects: the sharing of food, and the safety offered by a protected base camp" (1984, 340). Isaac's model only incorporated the first of these aspects, but does not consider the role of safety in interpreting hominid behavior. Surely, those hominids were constantly vigilant for their safety. Thus, by including the role of fear in hominid behavior, Potts offers a more empathic corrective to Isaac's food sharing model.

Stressing the element of safety, Potts revises Isaac's interpretation of the east African sites. Potts envisions three primary places involved in the hominid meat eating behavior. These are the kill site, a worksite, and a place where the food was consumed.

The kill site is the place where carrion was left behind by four legged predators. Potts, like Isaac, suggests that meat from big animals was more likely obtained from kills made by animal predators than from hominids hunting. Since these hominids were as yet unable to bring down large prey, the meat was probably scavenged after the killer ate its fill and abandoned the rest, or maybe the hominids scared it off.

The worksite is where the meat was taken from the kill site for butchering. Generally, the kill site would not be a safe place for the hominids to carve up their carrion. The lions, hyenas, or other large carnivore that made the kill might return and pounce upon one of the comparatively petite hominids. Hominids were also vulnerable to those smaller predators that travelled in packs, such as the African wild dogs. Such animals in the area may have heard the sounds of the kill, or have seen circling vultures, just as the scavenging hominids likely did, and also sought out the place as an opportunity for food. Thus, it would be unwise to linger in such an area.

The worksites are known to have a variety of stone tools that can be used for cutting, scraping, chopping, and cobble stones to use to knock sharp flakes off other stones. The early hominids could not carry all this equipment with them as they roamed in their core areas searching for food. So as a matter of convenience they would have a variety of worksites scattered around the lands they traversed. In this scenario, while wandering, a hominid would only have to carry one sharp stone flake for cutting. Those cutting implements would be useful for butchering carcasses, as well as for carving digging sticks, and for cutting vines, branches, and opening plant based foods, such as tubers dug out of the ground and too tough to bite into. When the hominids came across a fresh kill, they could quickly cut off large chunks and carry these to the cache of stone tools for further working. Potts finds that there is "no evidence that whole or nearly whole carcasses were transported to the [work] sites. Instead, it is primarily limb bones" (1984, 344).

But even these worksites were dangerous places for those who stayed too long. The smell of blood would likely have attracted hungry predators. Potts notes that the Olduvai sites have the bones of many smaller carnivores and those of some large ones as well. This suggests that some animals may have been attracted to the spots where hominids had been working on their treasures of meat only to be caught and killed by larger creatures. Indeed, some hominid bones have also been found at the worksites. That means they probably died there. One hominid skull was found with scratches of carnivore teeth marks on it (1984, 344).

Thus, the better part of valor would have been to cut off chunks of meat and pass them out quickly so the band members could carry their share away from that space to another area where it would be safer to sit and munch on their prize. And, as I mentioned above, chewing raw foods requires a long time. So sitting and eating at either a kill site or a butchering site for the time required to chew their raw food would be extremely risky.

We see, then, that taking a more empathic view, as Potts has done, can change the meaning of the evidence. Considering the need of the hominids for more personal safety, Isaac and the Leakeys can be understood as having excavated *worksites*, rather than "home bases." If such an inferred place is factually correct, then the meaning of the sites

Isaac called "home bases" requires rethinking.

A variety of stone tools may not have been needed at the safe consumption sites. Only a small sharp stone for slicing off chunks of meat to chew would be needed. The raw meat was likely carried to the site by hand, perhaps on a bed of leaves, or on a bark tray. Plant food to share may also have been carried there by the same type of degradable material. In this scenario, the bones and stone tools left at the worksites are the only artefacts that survived two million years of weathering. The third place, where the raw, uncooked food was shared has left no such enduring artifacts.

Social Life

Isaac's home base model envisions both a division of labor and hominids engaged in socializing during their communal feast. While Potts agrees that a cooperative ad hoc division of labor must have occurred at the Olduvai worksites, in his view, "it is not possible to assume that food-sharing [as in a common meal] ... occurred at the early sites at Olduvai. The available evidence suggests that hominids would have minimized the time spent at these sites, rather than having used them as the primary focus of social activity" (1984, 344-345). In other words, these worksites were not picnic areas, but more like crime scenes at which the time spent there is kept as brief as possible. Potts concludes that "the concentration of bones and stone tools do not represent fully formed campsites but an antecedent to them" (1984, 338).

Thus, we can imagine that when a recently killed hefty antelope carcass was discovered, a few members of the band would quickly cut off the meatiest sections, such as the legs, sides, and rump. They might have taken out inner parts as well. A cleaned stomach or bladder could be converted into a water jug. Perhaps they prized the heart or liver. They may have stripped off the hide to make carrying devices, bedding, or clothes. Potts speculates that sinew may have been cut out, presumably for later use as a kind of string (1984, 345).

Each of the strongest hominids would carry a hunk of meat to the nearest stone tool cache. There the meat would be carved into smaller chunks for distribution among the band members. While the butchers were at work, other band members might be busy gathering additional plant based foods in the anticipation of sharing these with the meat cutters. Then all would come together in a temporary campsite a safe distance from the worksite for a festive common meal. I imagine that the communal act of sharing food would likely have replicated in each band member the joyful experience of the original act of food sharing.

Yet, even the places where the hominids ate together were not "home bases." A day or two later, when the meat was gone, hominid life would have returned to "normal." That is, necessity would send them back to the old ways of self-feeding foraging with sharing as a convivial, but non-essential, activity. The division of labor that once served festive food sharing so well would dissolve until needed again.

Those hominids of 2mya could not stay in one place for long, both because they had to continually find fresh sources of plant based food, and so as to keep one step ahead of prowling predators. Nor would there have been the cultivation of a complex or sophisticated social life or culture beyond that which is possible for bands of foragers, like today's primates, which are perpetually on the go. Infants and children would have to be brought along. As a practical matter, it seems likely that any injured, ill, or infirm band members would have to keep up, or be left to die. That is what foraging primates do.

Stages in the use of Fire

Potts concludes that what Isaac called "home bases" were actually early stages in "a hypothetical course for the development of modern [hunter-gatherer style] home bases" (1984, 346). In his view, to become a safe place for food sharing, social life, child rearing, etc., hominids needed, among other things, "the controlled use of fire" (1984, 346). While modern hunter-gatherers process animal parts extensively, such as the San of Botswana boiling meat and bones, the old hominid sites "show no evidence of the complete processing of meat or bone" (1984, 344). Indeed, Potts notes that there is no evidence of fire use at these sites from 2mya; "Olduvai hominids lived, evidently, without fire" (1984, 344).

As I will discuss later, the knowledge of fire making was still a long way off. But once discovered, the knowledge of how to start and use campfires enabled the establishment of a regular division of labor, and facilitated the cultivation of the social, and political, activities that have developed in such home bases as those among contemporary hunter-gatherers. Informed by Potts's insights, we can understand that the sites Isaac referenced mark a transition period from self-feeding foragers, occasionally sharing food, to an eventual food sharing way of life in home bases. The latter, as we will see, is a necessary, but not quite sufficient, condition for the development of the first political system.

Rolland on Home Bases

As we have seen, scientists such as Binford and Potts have criticized Isaac's characterization of the two million year old sites in east Africa as "home bases." Yet another expert in the field, Nicolas Rolland (2004), has joined what he calls the "intense debates and diverging conclusions" about the existence and nature of such home bases (2004, 262-263). He is especially concerned with "arguments about whether earlier Lower Paleolithic occurrences (such as at Olduvai Gorge) could be distinguished … from pongid nesting sites; or that spatially fixed resource defended focal sites represented actual forerunners of Paleolithic home bases" (2004, 263 inner citations omitted).

Rolland, who is sensitive to the idea that hominid studies begin with the split, focuses on the evolutionary trends that follow thereafter in an effort to understand when hominid campsites can appropriately be deemed "home bases." He finds that along this evolutionary path there are several "emergent bio-behavioral traits that separated at a very early stage of evolution (between 6 and 4mya) [sic] ancient hominids from extant and, probably, all other fossil primate species" (2004, 259-260f).

Over this long stretch of time, these traits included bipedalism, an increasing taste for meat protein, increased tool making with stone and other materials such as wood and bone, and an increasingly complex exploitation of natural resources beyond mere foraging. In his view, these "traits contributed in making various aspects of hominid lifeways a unique adaptive niche that was increasingly divergent from those of their primate relatives, with the consequence that some of their behaviors become archaeologically more identifiable" (2004, 260-261).

Rolland finds that for their first few million years, the original hominids likely foraged in the day light hours, and then found a safe area in which to curl up and sleep when darkness came, just as contemporary primates do (2004. 262, 263). There may have been times when they tarried for a few days, in what Rolland calls "high biomass settings," before moving on. If so, this behavior would be less of a home base, and more analogous to "pongid nesting sites" (2004, 263).

A Safe Place to Sleep

Rolland, like Potts, incorporates an empathic understanding of the role fear likely played in hominid behavior. Also in agreement with Potts that the early hominids must have separated their eating place from their worksite, Rolland adds another possible fact. By the time the hominids had learned to butcher and eat meat in separate places, roughly 2mya, they would also have learned, possibly the hard way, that sleeping in the same place where they ate meat was also unsafe. The odor of the meat and bones and of the blood in the ground could attract carnivores, which might prey on a sleeping hominid. Therefore, on the occasions when they had meat, they likely ate it in one place, and then moved away from there to another place to sleep. Thus, besides the kill site and worksite mentioned by Isaac, and the eating area that Potts suggested was separated from the worksite, Rolland adds a fourth important place to the early hominid way of life – safe sleeping areas. At this stage in their development, then, those hominids had no place to call "home." They were always on the move.

The Punctuated Evolution of Fire Use

Like Potts, in Rolland's view, the time when hominids acquired the mastery of fire marked the turning point in "the shift from a core area system [of foraging] to a home base system" (2004, 259). While hominids may have taken advantage of fires caused by nature, like foraging for cooked plants and animals in burn areas, a time came when they learned to start their own fires at will. After this, they were able to form home bases. Because, as I mentioned above, home base living is a necessary, albeit not sufficient, condition for the emergence of the first political system, establishing where and when the regular use of campfires began will provide political science a clear idea of the origins of the first political system.

From Africa, through the Levant, into Europe, Eurasia, Australia, and China evidence has been found of the regular use of fire as the foundation for home base living. But this probably did not become a part of the hominid way of life all over the world all at once. Instead, the practice more likely emerged in different times and places as "a punctuated event" (2004, 256, 259, 253). Thus, a "major, multistage transformation separated higher primate single-night or shorter duration nonrecurrent nesting sites from the fixed-point recurrent Paleolithic home bases of hominids" (2004, 260-261). Aware that opinions differ, Rolland finds that "there is secure evidence for anthropogenic fire clusters by later Middle Pleistocene times (400- 350kya)" (2004, 252, 253, 259, 270).[12] Indeed, he adds, that actual home base sites begin appearing in the record "around 400kya," in the same time range as the regular use of fire (2004, 270).[13]

Finding Hearths

Identifying campfire-centered home bases requires painstaking, expert excavation. According to Rolland, the best evidence of regular fire use is spaces that were clearly designed for the use of fire. These can include a circle of stone, a dugout, a concentration of ashes or charcoal, burnt bones or stones, patches of burnt soil, or other indications of hearths (2004, 263). One challenge for researchers is to distinguish between deliberate behavior and the natural occurrences of fire, such as a burnt tree trunk left by a wildfire. Wind and rushing water can put items together which give the false appearance of deliberate fire use.

Rolland reports that at least 60 sites with probable evidence of deliberate fire use have been found (2004, Table 3). These sites range from east Africa, China and other places in Asia, and in both western and eastern Europe. He notes that the places that have been excavated most thoroughly, for example France, have the higher numbers of sites with probable evidence of regular fire use in the range of from 400-350kya. Further excavations will likely uncover other places in the world with persuasive evidence of controlled fire use. Precise times for the first use of fire at will are unlikely to ever be known because of the ambiguity of the evidence. Rolland discounts the speculations that such fire use became a regular practice prior to the period he mentions. "It is noteworthy that few, if any, of the best known Lower Paleolithic occurrences older than 600-500kya from Africa, Asia, or especially Europe contain unambiguous anthropogenic fire traces (such as ashes, charcoal, burnt bones or stones, or hearths)" (2004, 253).

Home Base Culture

Hominid life, in Rolland's view, then, was probably sustained by self-feeding foraging, with occasional food sharing, from the time of the split, roughly 6mya, until they learned to master fire, as recently as 400kya. In other words, the transition from self-feeding foraging to a fully food sharing way of life spanned about five and one half million years. The move from the temporary sites of 2mya, discussed by Isaac and Potts, took nearly one and a half million years to become true home bases.

With good reason, then, Rolland declares this fire centered home base living to be "an adaptive breakthrough" (2004, 270). Thereafter, the evidence of hominid fire use, and their numerous and varied other artifacts, "reveal an accelerating dependence on a richer, more specialized cultural 'margin'" (2004, 270). For example, of the four types of places that distinguished hominid life prior to the mastery of fire – kill site, worksite, eating site, and sleeping site – the latter three would be merged into the home base.

Because campfires served as a deterrent to predator invasions of hominid encampments, the hominids could eat meat, when they had it, in the same campsite where they slept. Campfires would enable the hominids to stay up after dark, rather than retiring at dusk (2004, 264). Hence, notes Rolland, the "shift to home bases entailed a major reorganization of the day and night arrangement of ancient hominid lifeways, and thereby a further divergence from pongid or ground-living primates' land use patterns" (2004, 264). Among other things, socializing around the campfire likely enhanced bonding, and facilitated language use and the making of cultures (2004, 250). Hunting may have increased as a consequence of home base living. The home base provides a center of operations for strategic planning, a work place where community synergies can increase the sophistication of tools and weaponry, and campfires raise the value of fresh meat for cooking.

The Theory of Hominid Nature

While Rolland does not explicitly discuss the theory of the hominid self-bred food sharing nature offered here, he agreed with Isaac's understanding of the hominids as more prone to share food than other creatures. Rolland's observations make it clear that the home base provided enormously expanded opportunities for a creature that desired to share food. His research shows that, in the transition, home bases would tend to be "sites strategically located for resource exploitation by local groups of food-sharing foragers" (2004, 262). He writes that by the Middle Paleolithic (around 400kya), the home base was well on its way to becoming "the place where animal and vegetal foods are introduced, *shared*, and consumed" (2004, 263 italics added).

As the transition progressed, home bases would also have become "a setting favoring the transmission of knowledge and behaviors through prolonged learning by the young of shared and transmitted technical, socio-economic, and cognitive repertoires necessary for ensuring group survival" (2004, 263). Home bases would also provide for the "protection of juvenile and defenseless individuals against natural elements and predation" (2004, 263). Such, then, was pre-Homo sapiens, hominid civilization.

Constructing the First Political System

To call the first home bases, as did Rolland, "an adaptive breakthrough," seems to me to be an understatement. This was a monumental achievement, five and a half million years in the making. Without the founding of the first home bases, society, organized beyond the primate level, would probably never have happened. This accomplishment was due, in large part, to the hominid self-bred desire to share food. Without that desire, none of them would have recognized, much less seized, the opportunity the mastery of fire had given them. Creating the first home base enabled an incomparable revolutionary change from primate level self-feeding foraging to a fully food sharing civilization.

The first home base was little more than a campfire around which pre-human creatures sat and ate the food items they had brought in to share together. There was likely some lag of time from when they learned to start a fire at will, and when they learned to use it for cooking. Before then, they would have munched on raw food in the glow and safety of the fire. Already, however, they would have had a division of labor without which the home base could not survive.

Self-feeding foragers need almost no supervision, or leadership, to carry on in their way of life. The chimpanzee Alpha male does little more than protect his harem, break up fights, and decide when it is time for the troop to move along within their territory (de Waal 1998, 168-188). But for a home base to continue as a reliable, life sustaining institution, deliberate measures must be taken to maintain and preserve it. There must be a division of labor consisting of defined tasks, carried out on a regular basis. Without that, hominid life would revert back to the primate level. Those hominids had to somehow decide, in the words of Harold Lasswell (1936), "who gets what, when, and how?"

What, then, was the political culture like for the hominids who achieved the formation of the first home bases, and found ways to sustain them? What kind of rules would likely be made by a creature with a strong desire to share food with his fellows? And how were such rules likely enforced? It is, of course, in the making and enforcing of such rules that the first political system arises.

One principle of interpretation to apply in this case is that the rules these hominids made were probably reflections of their nature. We have seen that in the five and a half million years since the split, at least one lineage of hominid persisted in the practice of preferring food sharing individuals for mating. This was probably far from a uniform practice, but more like a slight tendency gradually increasing over that long stretch of time. But after the first home bases were fashioned so as to further food sharing, the importance of the former tendency would likely have become a guiding principle in the selection of mating partners.

The clear function of this principle would be to reproduce offspring who, when mature, would have a desire to share food as a central aspect of their character. Without the continuous birthing of individuals of such character, the home base social organization would be much more difficult to achieve, and would be unlikely to persist. Thus, another principle of interpretation is that creatures with a strong desire to share food will probably be very cooperative in coordinating their behavior to satisfy that end. The individualism and immediate gratification practiced by self-feeding foragers would not likely have lent itself to fashioning the high degrees of social organization required for home base living.

Self-feeding foragers have no reason to build a campfire. They simply move about consuming the raw food they acquire by their own efforts. But without a campfire, a home base could not be set up as the central gathering place for food sharing creatures. Thus, rules must be made on this account. Specific tasks had to be performed regularly to keep the campfire burning. First, someone must take on the responsibility to start the fire. Then, that person or another must stay there and tend to it. Such individuals must forego foraging while trusting others to bring in food to share with them. New fuel, and in the right amount, must continually be fed the fire to keep it burning. Other band members must go out and find the right kind of fuel, gather it, and carry it back in a timely fashion. They, too, must forego self-feeding foraging. Even before cooking, these tasks had to be carried out so as to have a campfire.

At this point, then, the hominids are steeped in a condition where values must be allocated. If food sharing is valued, then a specific division of labor, far beyond self-feeding, is indispensable. The decisions must be made as to which individuals, or small groups, will do what tasks. Therefore, a clear, policy making and enforcement process must be instituted which would be accepted as authoritative by at least the greater part of the band, if not the whole. For the first time in the history of the universe, as far as anyone knows, all sorts of political lessons would have to be learned by these relatively small brained hominids. How could this first political system have functioned?

More than likely, authority was vested in some of the elders of the band. Each child would have grown up depending upon the guidance of their elders, and have learned to trust their judgment. The elders would likely have conferred with one another as to the basic tasks that were necessary to continue the food sharing way of life. Although lacking sophisticated language, and the capacity for highly abstract thought, they would have understood that they had a common desire to live in a food sharing community, and they would have learned, perhaps with some trial and error, what sorts of practical actions were necessary to achieve their shared purpose.

Because their characters were naturally oriented towards sharing food, it seems safe to assume they shared political authority as well. Class domination seems highly unlikely in this stage of history. Class domination requires ownership and control of the means of production by a few who can compel the many to serve them. But these were probably not the conditions of the first hominids living in home bases for the purpose of sharing food. Political authority was probably widely shared. To this day, contemporary hunter-gatherers are largely egalitarian (von Rueden, 2014; Service 1975; Boehm 1993).

As Potts noted, caches of stone tools were left in places around the hominid foraging range. They were in use for many years, and sat there for millions of years. Various bands and succeeding generations likely used these tools as needed, and left them in place, where they could be used again. This strongly suggests an absence of any ego-centric belief in the abstract notion of "private property." In other words, an ancient pro-group, selfless ethic of sharing probably extended to tools, food, and political authority.

After conferring about what work needs to be done, the elders may have asked for volunteers, or else assigned tasks. They would have known which individuals were best suited to do the various kinds of work. Those who were best able to start campfires would likely be assigned that task. There is no reason to suppose that a male would be any more able than a female to be in charge of starting and maintaining a fire. Indeed, while women were surely capable of hunting and gathering tasks, those who were mothers with dependent children might have been the best choice for managing the campfire during the day. (Having the knowledge of how to start a campfire, a continuous fire may not have been necessary.) Perhaps in the evenings all interested parties would have participated in the discussions about the future needs of the community, such as what the needs were for keeping up the fires. The elders would have to assign the tasks of gathering firewood and other combustible material to specific individuals. If there were 50 members of a band, they probably needed more than one campfire for heat, light, and later, cooking.

While some types of produce can be stored in the ground, or in baskets, other types of food are more perishable, particularly meat. The elders would have to be informed about inventories. So that everyone did not go out in the morning and start collecting the same kind of unneeded foods, work assignments would have to be made on the bases of community need and individual ability to complete the tasks. Some would chop wood, others carry water. Perhaps they followed the principle of "from each according to his ability, to each according to his need."[14]

How would a community of creatures whose nature it is to want to share food with one another likely enforce the authoritative allocation of tasks and values? Would these hominids be more likely to form a dictatorship based on force and violence, or more likely to use shame and moral suasion to enforce order? I lean towards the latter interpretation.[15]

Also, there would have been other situations in which enforcement would be required. Since different work groups and individuals would be bringing in a variety of food items for the community to share, how would disputes over who gets what, when, and how, be settled?

Besides the problems of distributive justice, there were likely issues of criminal justice. Suppose bullying, rape, or murder occurred? Depending on the problem, a range of techniques were likely employed. Perhaps perpetual freeloaders, serious nuisances, and violent offenders would be banished. These creatures, like all social animals, probably had to find ways to deal with disturbances of the peace due to flare-ups of strong emotions like resentment, jealousy, and murderous rage.

If these were the kinds of issues hominids had to deal with in the first campfire-centered home bases, before they learned about regular cooking, then they surely had to continue finding ways to keep order after cooking began. Peacefully parceling out chunks of roasted meat to hungry hominids after a hard day's work, was likely a challenge to their political ingenuity.[16]

As the authorities made policy for the whole band, they would have received feedback regarding the success and wisdom of their decisions. Were they assigning a sufficient number of helpers to the fire keeping moms? Did the older children they sent out for water need more adult protection? In order to keep the peace, and assure the persistence of their way of life, they would have probably made the necessary adjustments in response to the input from members of the community.

While we cannot know the specifics of what they did, we do know that they were able to manage their political challenges. Their way of life was successful for hundreds of thousands of years leading up to the Agricultural Revolution, beginning roughly 12-10kya. Indeed, the whole history of human civilization emerged out of the political system first forged by these food sharing hominids.

Although these hominids had long been mating with partners selected, at least in part, for their food sharing qualities, reproduction is not always uniform. That is, while a male and female might both have the dominant genes for food sharing, and behave accordingly, one or both might have recessive genes carried over from the selfish days of self-feeding foraging. Thus, it would have regularly happened that some offspring would grow to become more selfish than their brothers and sisters. This fact of population genetics would ensure, along with the necessities of life, that an effective political system for the authoritative allocation of values and enforcement of rules would continue to be necessary.

Conclusion: The Loss of Selflessness

In the modern world of 193 nations in the United Nations, one might reasonably suspect that at least in some of these nations, the genetic sequence favoring food sharing behavior has lost its efficacy, and the desire to live to share food has faded from the psychology of the folks living in such places. Be that as it may, the propensity to live in a political system – that is, in a process for the authoritative allocation of values for a society – has carried over despite the changes in the underlying political environment. Indeed, the old hominid-made pattern has proven so adaptable that some four hundred thousand years after its creation, it is flourishing.

Endnotes

1. This chapter was first posted at the American Political Science Association Preprint Program site in 2020 at,
https://preprints.apsanet.org/engage/apsa/article-details/5f4817b9572c8200124a3cdd

2. Easton was APSA president from 1968 to 1969. His primary works explaining his theory are, 1953, 1965a, and 1965b. Some of the chief misunderstandings of Easton's theory of the political system are criticized in Kelleher 2017.

3. See the United Nations "about" webpage at, https://www.un.org/en/about-un/.

4. Writing a literature review in the late 1950s, Easton observed that the field of "political anthropology," applying his conception of the political system, "does not yet exist and will not exist until a great many conceptual problems are solved." (1959, 210) Assessing whether that is still true is beyond the scope of the instant essay, but see Arnoff and Kubik 2013.

5. The broad consensus among scientists is that Homo sapiens emerged in the region of east Africa between 150,000 and 200,000 years ago. But opinion is not unanimous as to either time or place. Arguments have been made that Homo sapiens first emerged in Europe, or North Africa, or Asia, or in these and other places both independently and simultaneously – the "multiregional theory." Skull and bone fragments recently found in Morocco are said to show Homo sapiens evolved over 300,000 years ago. But DNA tests have not been run on those skeletal remains. For a review of the issues, with links, see Callaway 2017. Fortunately, political science does not have to either settle this debate or await its settlement before presenting the evidence for the origins of the first political system. (As we will see, Homo sapiens inherited the first political system from their hominid ancestors.)

6. For a more recent account of chimp food sharing, see de Waal, ed. 2001, Chapter Four.

7. Kelleher 2016 examines de Waal's claims (at 1998) for chimp "political" behavior, and finds that this does not rise to the level of a political system, as defined by Easton.

8. For an example of the disagreement between geneticists compare Patterson 2006 and Barton 2006.

9. The cartoonish image of a neat progression from a monkey evolving into an American businessman carrying his briefcase has probably done more harm than good for the understanding of human evolution.

10. For interpretivists, "that past as in fact it occurred" cannot be known. Only interpretations of the past can be known. These derive their validity from the

consensus of the informed community. Binford's positivism would also find it difficult to acknowledge that pre-human hominids were sentient beings, and he would therefore be skeptical that the feelings or motivations of such distant creatures could ever be known. Indeed, in the extreme, as the old joke goes, one positivist in a lab would stare at his colleague and wonder if he is sentient. Rejecting positivist dogmatics, empathy must assume that genetically close living organisms have a similar consciousness and some similarities of emotions and experience. This point is further argued by biologist, Marc Bekoff 2013. Cf. Low 2012. Also see, "Animal Consciousness."
https://en.wikipedia.org/wiki/Animal_consciousness

[11] While Potts focuses on Olduvai Gorge and does not discuss evidence from Koobi Fora, as Isaac did, Potts's arguments are not undermined by the omission.

[12] Here, Rolland stretches the meaning of "anthropogenic" to include pre-human hominids.

[13] In accord: Gowlett and Wrangham 2013, Gowlett 2016; Roebroeks and Villa 2011; Wrangham and Carmody 2010; Wrangham 2009, 2017.

[14] Karl Marx's term "Primitive Communism" seems an apt appellation for the food sharing model.

[15] While all the experts I rely on reject the "Killer Ape" theory of hominid nature (as popularized by Ardrey 1961), in the field of hominid studies a few dramatists keep it alive in various forms. Gintis 2000, 2019 speculates that because every hominid had his own "lethal weapons" with which to slay individuals seeking the Alpha position, their political organizations were egalitarian and cooperation was based on a kind of Hobbesian social contract, stemming from mutual fear. Wrangham 1996, much more of a showman, fantasizes that after learning to cook, hominid males brutally enslaved their women, like a gang of sociopathic Alley Oops.

[16] Wrangham (2017) has another, perhaps more realistic, proposal. He argues that after cooking became a regular practice, pre-humans evolved to become physiologically dependent upon having cooked food in their diet, and Homo sapiens have inherited that dependency. He argues that modern humans cannot survive on a diet of only raw food. If this is true, then a political system dedicated to preserving the cooked food way of life, including its entire supply chain, is now essential to the survival of the species. Returning back to self-feeding foraging on raw foods in the woodlands and savannas of Africa is not an option for humanity, as it once was to the early hominids.

74

Chapter Three:

How to Measure the Goodness of a Political System

Introduction: Easton Meets Hartman

"Normative Political Science," as I use the term, is based on David Easton's theory of the political system combined with Robert S. Hartman's philosophy of value science.[1] Hartman's half of the synthesis is presented in his main work, *The Structure of Value*.[2] In that book, Hartman introduced the fundamental principles of "value science." Of course, the term "value" has many usages. In economics it can refer to the price of something, or a bargain, etc. Information of interest to someone can be called "valuable information." A person may rank his or her favorite music, indicating how he or she "values" the various recordings. The term "value" can be used as an alternate to the word "desire." Thus, objects of desire, or want, even like or dislike, can be referred to as the way objects are valued. In ordinary usage, "values" can be a person's ethical, moral, or political principles.

But in Hartman's special use, the term "value," like the term "goodness," refers to the measurement of a thing according to how well it fulfills the definition of its concept. A thing's "value," then, depends on the degree to which it fills the definition of the concept, or category, for it. The assessment of how well a thing fulfills the category for it employs what I call "the Logic of Assessment." That is, each element of the definition is compared to the corresponding part of the actual item being assessed. The differences and similarities are noted. The result is its "value," or goodness.

In the Introduction to the present book, we discussed some examples of the Logic of Assessment. Suppose a botanist has in mind the definition of the scientific concept for a rose. Each particular flower is unique, and so fulfills that definition in its own measure. If the specimen meets the basic requirement for membership in that category it is a "good" rose. To be more thorough she may also record in her notes how the thing lacks some properties of the category, or has some excellent examples of other properties, for example, richness of color.

To take another example, a "pachyderm" with only three legs and an illness is still an elephant, but not as good an elephant as healthy four legged members of the category. Thus, taking the measurement of how well a real thing actually fulfills the elements of its category is entirely an empirical exercise. Also, the key elements of a definition can be numbered. For example, a "pachyderm" can be defined as 1) a healthy organism with 2) a trunk, 3) a large round body, 4) four legs, and 5) a tail. If the specimen under consideration has all five elements, then it is a good pachyderm. Of course, there is no end to the complexity of measurement that is possible in this system. The ability for assessing goodness with mathematical precision makes the method "scientific." This is, in large part, why Hartman argues that a "science" of value is possible.

Easton's concern was different than Hartman's. Easton wanted to establish political science as an empirical social science that studies the political system. In his view, political science attempts to *explain* how a particular political system is able to meet the challenges in its environment and sustain itself, or "persist."[3] We will see that Easton's theory of the political system, which he intended to be used as an interpretive framework, or norm, guiding research, can also be used as a standard, or norm, by which to assess or evaluate the performance of a political system.[4] These are the two *normative* uses of Easton's concept of the political system. By bringing in Hartman, Normative Political Science takes Easton's great work into a new realm – *from explanatory to evaluational*.

The evaluation side of Normative Political Science, among other things, asks the question, "What is a good political system?" The central theme of this chapter will be to explain how that question can be addressed. Following Hartman's pioneering work, I will use the term "good" not in a moral sense, but in the scientific sense of measurement. I will discuss how, using Easton's theory of the political system, taking the measure of goodness can be practiced in political science. We will see how the goodness of a political system can be assessed as excellent, adequate, or poor. Then, as with roses or elephants, political systems can be compared as best, better, worse, or worst. In the Conclusion of this book, I will explain how, once the measure of a system's goodness has been taken, those areas which are found to be faulty can be diagnosed to discover the causes of their under par performances. This would set the stage for suggesting remedies to improve the performance of the political system, or its under-performing parts.

In the application of Hartman's value science there are three dimensions of goodness to be considered. Hartman calls these the systemic, the extrinsic, and the intrinsic. Each of these dimensions will be discussed in this chapter.[5]

The Flow Chart for Explanatory Political Science

For Easton, political science is the study of the political system.[6] In brief, as I discussed in Chapter One, Easton defines the political system as an emergent property of that behavior which is undertaken in relation to the authoritative allocation of values for a society. Thus he identifies "a political system as those patterns of interaction through which values [such as desired things or principles] are allocated for a society and these allocations are accepted as authoritative by most persons in the society most of the time."[7] Political science "would thus seek to understand that system of interactions in any society through which such binding or authoritative allocations are made and implemented."[8] While Easton may use various formulations for his conception of a political system, he presents a Flow Chart which serves as an unambiguous illustration of his concept of the political system. [9]

FLOW CHART

Inputs (as supports or demands) –> Conversion process –> Outputs (as laws, policies, implementation, etc.) –> Feedback (returning as Inputs) from the Environment –>

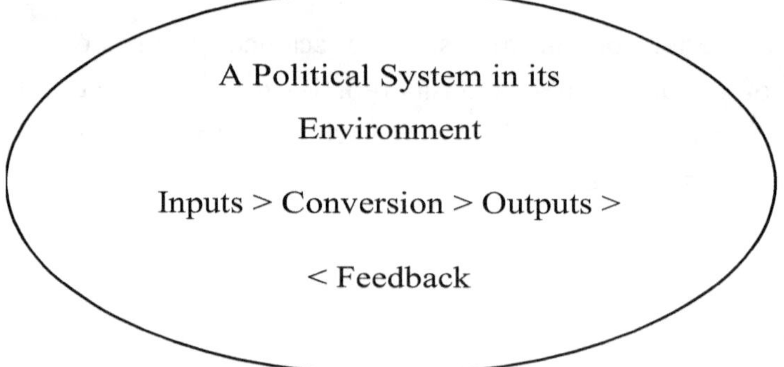

"Values," in Easton's definition of the political system, are objects of desire, want, or interest, and are indicated in a political system primarily by the demands and supports coming from members of the system.[10] These are inputs into the conversion process. In that process, the expressed values are turned into legislation and government policy by the authorities. Laws and policies are the primary outputs of the conversion process. Those are the authoritatively allocated values. These outputs go into the environment, which includes the system's membership, the natural environment, and foreign political systems. From the environment, further inputs are made. These may be original inputs, or feedback as responses to outputs. This is a dynamic system in constant interaction with its environment.

Complexity and Flow

The lines of flow represent the decisions and actions taken in the political process as information moving through the system. The diagram here depicts the most simplified statement of how a political system carries out the authoritative allocation of values. But Easton also uses much more complex models in his written work.[11] There is probably no limit to how complex a flow chart can be made. Considering the plethora of political actors and institutions in most political systems, the only limit on how complex a model of a political system can be is how complex a researcher wants to make it. (The assessment of a system's goodness can be equally complex.)

Continuous Flow

Easton advises political scientists that his approach "enables and indeed compels us to analyze a political system in dynamic terms."[12] Each stage in the process sends information to the next one in "a continuous never-ending flow."[13] The "continuous flow of the interrelated activities through which a political system persists" models the political system in action.[14] Thus, the study of political systems entails the "need to interpret political processes as a continuous and interlinked flow of behavior."[15]

Unique v Uniform

Easton intended his definition of the political system to be a uniform interpretive framework around which to organize political science research.[16] Organizing the study of a political system according to the Flow Chart guides the researcher to the relevant aspects of the system. As the Chart shows, the elements, or "internal variables," of a political system are inputs, conversion, outputs, and feedback, all interacting with the system's environment. With these categories in mind, the researcher can begin her or his study of a system by looking for the behavior patterns that fit the categories. Easton notes that the elements of the Flow Chart can be conveniently used by a researcher "to begin plugging in the complexities of political life."[17]

This will enable an orderly description of a particular political system as it is in operation. For Easton, explanatory political science is "primarily concerned with understanding and explaining [how these variables] function, the stresses imposed upon them, and the behavior that occurs as a response to such stress."[18] Because in practice every political system is unique, the primary question for researchers is as to how this particular political system manages to cope with its stresses, and survive, or persist.

While every behavioral political system is different, and always changing, the scientific approach to the study of each system remains uniform because it is based on the conceptual, or theoretical model of the political system. Thus the Flow Chart model can be used as an aid to identify and explain political behavior in all the varieties of it that the world has to offer. Because Easton's interpretive framework gives focus and structure to the study of political systems, the profession can accumulate a body of methodologically related data, insights, and principles, i.e., political science knowledge.

Political Life and Biology

As mentioned in Chapter One, Easton envisions the political system as the central form of "political life." By "life," he means the biological process of living, "what we may call the fundamental life processes of a political system."[19] However, he understands the political system not as an organism, but as an organization by which humans live. Thus, he conceives of "political life as a system of behavior."[20]

As a system for sustaining the orderly authoritative allocation of values in a society, the political system tends to respond to challenges, whether internal or external, by producing laws and policies, or taking other actions, that will favor its own survival, or persistence, in its environment. But the actors, whose behavior constitutes the political system, act with considerable agency and responsibility, and are not like particles or other lifeless objects which behave more in accordance with mechanical principles. The "politically relevant actors" tend to act with the shared intention, or set of meanings, to keep their system a going concern. Thus a system's persistence depends, in large part, on "the capacity of a system [through its political actors] to take constructive actions [which] seek to adapt or to cope with possible stress."[21]

Flow and the Form of Government

What matters most for explanatory political science, in Easton's view, is not what form of government a system takes, but to understand how the input/output process enables a system to meet the challenges in its environment. That is why, for Easton, asking how a system is able to maintain its "persistence through change ... [and] over time ... has seemed to be the most inclusive kind of question that one might ask about a political system."[22] Indeed, "the primary goal of [explanatory] political analysis is to understand how political systems manage to persist through time."[23] The institutions and the form of government in a society are only the means by which that process operates. Easton intends his Flow Chart to be a model for all types of governmental organizations, including democracy, autocracy, etc. "The existence of extreme variations in political structures in political systems, ranging from the most democratic to the most totalitarian, does not prevent the operation of this [input/output] process."[24] The Flow Chart highlights "the processes that all types of political systems share and that make it possible for them to cope, however successfully, with stresses that threaten to destroy the capacity of a society to sustain any political system at all."[25]

Conflict and Scarcity

In Easton's view, the "fundamental fact confronting all societies is that scarcity of some valued things prevails. It leads inevitably to disputes over their allocation."[26] One important function for the political system is to authoritatively manage "the conflicting demands over scarce values."[27] Also, "every society provides" ways to deal with behavior "perceived to be excessively disruptive of the prevailing ideas of order and justice."[28] In Easton's view, "no society could survive without providing for some processes through which authoritative allocations could be made, if and when differences arise with regard to valued things."[29] Generally, then, as we saw in Chapter Two, a political system will deal with "the major problems of a shared existence."[30]

Stress and the Fear of Death

The survival of a system is not, of course, a certainty. It "will depend upon the ability of the members of the system to deal with the conditions creating … stress."[31] Significant stress can result from events "that threaten to prevent a system from functioning."[32] Persistence, then, is *a collective human achievement* resulting from the energy and political talent of a political leadership and their people. One of the hazards confronting political life is that unhelpful, even self-destructive, behavior is also possible. Hence, the risk of failure, or the death of a system, can add an element of drama to political science narratives. Easton comments that the "ability of some kind of political system to endure in a society might be something to gaze at with wonder had we not come to take it so much for granted as the normal course of things."[33]

The Two Kinds of Political System

Some of what we said in Chapter One bears repeating in order to set up the message here in Chapter Three. We said, for instance, that Easton uses the concept of the political system "in two different but related senses."[34] One usage is in reference to the actual "empirical behavior which we observe and characterize as political life [and that] as students of politics, we wish to understand and explain. We can speak of this phenomenal reality as the empirical or behaving system."[35] This behavioral political system is political life in action, struggling for survival, or persistence, in its environment. In Chapter Two we saw how the first behavioral political system may have emerged in the course of human evolution.

Easton writes that his other usage of the term is in reference to the symbolic construct, theoretical framework, or definition of "the political system" as patterns of interaction undertaken in relation to the authoritative allocation of values for a society. As I have suggested, this *concept* of the political system is most clearly represented by the Flow Chart. As a heuristic model, this conceptual political system "corresponds to the behaving system which it is designed to explain."[36] Easton insists that it "is of the utmost importance to keep these two kinds of systems distinct."[37]

Therefore, in the following discussion I will closely adhere to Easton's edict to keep the two definitions distinct. However, I will use the conceptual political system as *a standard* by which to measure the goodness of any behavioral political system. This is an innovation in the use of Easton's political theory because it was his intention only to shape the *explanatory* methods of political science. That is why he also noted that "Ethical evaluation and empirical explanation involve two different kinds of propositions that, for the sake of clarity, should be kept distinct."[38] He was unaware of Hartman's definition of "goodness" as scientific, or operational, rather than ethical or moral. As we will now see, using the conceptual political system to assess the goodness of a behavioral political system is not at all a venture into "ethical" speculation because it is wholly non-prescriptive, and strictly descriptive. Making these factual measurements is the task of *evaluative* political science, the other half of the Normative Political Science paradigm.

The Four Steps for Assessing the Goodness of a Political System

Going beyond the strictly explanatory purpose he intended for it, let us consider how Easton's interpretive framework can be used as a standard for assessing the goodness of a behavioral political system. As I have said, in Hartman's approach to assessing a thing's goodness there are three basic dimensions to be considered: the systemic, the extrinsic, and the intrinsic. After considering these three dimensions separately, the political scientist will be in a position to take a fourth step; that is, to render an over-all, or general, rating of a political system *as a whole*. This can be done individually, or comparatively. The special problems concerning the fourth step will be discussed towards the end of this essay.

The Systemic Dimension

In the first step of evaluation, the political scientist identifies the set of behaviors that he or she wants to study *as a political system*. The question is, can this set of social interactions reasonably be said to constitute an actual political system, and not something else, such as a mere collection of people milling about. As Easton notes, "the identification of a political system is a way of referring to those processes through which authoritative allocations are provided for ... the society."[39] This is a problem of categorizing. We have seen some examples of classifying things according to their appropriate category. For instance, a rose, elephant, or political system.

In most cases identifying a behavioral political system will be a routine matter. But sometimes the behavior on the ground may not be easily identified as having all the elements required to fit the category "political system." In some cases, as Easton notes, the question may be whether one or more of the essential variables, or functions, "has dropped below some critical point."[40] Suppose, for example, that the allocation of values, by legislation or through the courts, etc., are not accepted as authoritative or binding by a critical mass of the population. "Beyond that point the system disappears since it is no longer minimally effective."[41] What that "critical point" is will vary, and can only be identified by the study of a particular set of social interactions.

The identification of a political system does not require the full compliance of the entire population with the directives of the authorities. Easton notes that "compliance will vary on a continuum."[42] Even where there is dissent, if it is more likely than not that most members of a system will respect and obey the authorities, then a minimally functioning system can be classified as a "political system," the object of study for political science. In Easton's words, "The operation of essential variables need not be an all or nothing matter. ... The behavior involved varies on a range of effectiveness, and within that range a system may be able to persist."[43] If a society breaks down, and there is no central organization to allocate values, then there is no political system. A systemically good political system, then, is one which has an amount of political behavior that at least minimally satisfies each of the basic requirements of Easton's definition of a political system.

Suppose that the patterns of behavior in a location show extreme political disorder. Maybe armed gangs are fighting over the control of the government. Rather than values being allocated in an orderly and authoritative fashion, gang members might be grabbing what they can, forcing captives to work, and killing anyone who protests. Such conditions might qualify as being a kind of pre-political system, or in a state of civil war, or of descending into a failed state, but not as a "political system."[44] Warring gangs cannot be classified as allocating values for a society in an orderly and authoritative fashion. Currently, Haiti and Sudan can be seen as borderline example.

One question that might be of interest in the classifying process is whether this prospective "political system" is coming or going? That is, is the collective behavior under study a possible political organization emerging from a pre-political system condition, or is it descending towards a failed state? Also, a political system can vanish if it is conquered or colonized.

What Persists?

Generally, what "persists" is some form of the orderly allocation of values by authorities. Easton remarks that "a system can be said to persist even if it changes."[45] He means that if institutional alterations in a political system are made, for example, so as to adapt to environmental changes, the new arrangement can still be a political system. For instance, FDR's New Deal resulted in the establishment of several new institutions in the process of adapting to the system-threatening conditions of the Great Depression, but "the American political system" continued. Considering the historical record, Easton observes that "surprisingly few societies have succumbed because of their inability to provide some kind of structures and processes for the authoritative allocation of values."[46] Thus, the form of government may not persist, but the orderly allocation of values for the society can persist through changes in the form of government.[47]

A study as to why a given performance, or set of political behaviors, fails to qualify as a political system could make an interesting paper in itself. But once the patterns of interaction under study have been categorized as a "political system," then, in the next two steps, the system can be examined more closely to assess its operational goodness.

Assessing Operational and Intrinsic Goodness

Interactions rising to the level of a political system are a collective achievement; a performance of human initiative and cooperation that history shows can fail. For evaluative political science, as we have seen, at the first step, the problem is only to check whether some semblance of each function in the definition of the concept "political system" can be observed so as to justify the classification of the behavior as a "political system." The second step is to assess how well these essential functions are being carried out.

An evaluative political science study would begin, then, at the systemic level, with the political scientist making a case for his or her classification of a given set of behavior as in or out of the category "political system." Once certified, a behavioral political system can then be assessed for its degree of "operational goodness," and for its degree of "intrinsic goodness." From the point of view of Normative Political Science, at the extrinsic level, a political system is *operationally good* when it functions according to the specifications set for it in Easton's definition, exemplified by the Flow Chart. The more it fulfills those expectations, the better it is. The *intrinsic goodness* of a behavioral political system is assessed by what Easton calls the "political contentment" of its members. Intrinsic goodness will be explained further after the discussion of operational goodness.

The Importance of Persistence in Evaluation

As we know, for Easton, one of the core tasks of explanatory political science is to try to understand and explain how a particular behavioral political system is able to persist in its environment. However, for *evaluative* political science, persistence, in itself, is not a significant measure of a behavioral political system's goodness. This is because persistence is *prima facie* established when the initial determination is made that the set of behaviors of interest actually rise to the level of a political system. By definition, an existing political system is a persisting political system. While persistence is a core conception for explanatory political science, it can be given very little consideration after the first step of evaluative political science – the identification of an existing political system.

Persistence can proceed no matter how well a system operates. Even an inept system can persist by luck. An oppressive dictatorship may be able to persist just as long as a liberal democracy, perhaps longer. Indeed, while an operationally good political system will likely persist, as with people, bad things can happen to good political systems.

For example, the Mount Vesuvius volcano destroyed the political system in the ancient Roman city of Pompeii when it erupted in 79 AD and buried the city under a thick carpet of volcanic ash. The political system of the ancient Maya civilization in Mesoamerica existed between 2600 BC and 1200 AD when it collapsed, perhaps due to a prolonged draught. Conquest and occupation by an invading army can result in the destruction and replacement of a once operational political system. So, operational goodness is no guarantee of persistence, just as persistence is no guarantee of operational goodness.

The Starting Point for Evaluation

To start the study of a political system, one must select a point at which to begin. However, all functions are part of a dynamic process, and they will likely have overlap and intermingling. There is no starting point in an actual political system. As the Ancient Greek philosopher, Heraclitus, has reportedly observed, one cannot step into the same river twice.

Not only are the parts of the political system always on the go, no one can observe all of the infinite variables at work. Only gross features can be isolated for analysis. For instance, every person along the path of policy making has a unique set of understandings and motivations. These are factors in the political process; however, neither a god, nor a La Placean Mind, nor a supercomputer could take all such factors into account in an effort to explain an election, a piece of legislation, or other political event. Judgment with both talent and training is required to cut into the moving, indeed, creatively unfolding, jumble of factors that is politics. Political science is not for the mind that seeks simplicity.[48]

So, as the collective behavior carries on, the political scientist selects the relevant parts according to the type of evaluative study he or she has planned. Suppose the process of "allocation" is the subject of study. How well is allocation being carried out? Allocation can be seen as an output following the decision making done during the conversion phase. That phase can be seen as following upon particular inputs, such as demands for legislation favoring some group in the society. Allocation is also the subject upon which feedback may be given as subsequent input. Presumably, if allocating is being done well, the authorities will receive approving and supportive feedback.

Suppose the "authoritative" aspect is to be studied. In brief, authority is a type of social status, or legitimacy, given officials by the members of a political system. The meaning of "authority" within a system is contained in the political culture, or "regime," within the system's environment. Thus, it can be seen as a supportive input from the political environment. Authority can be acknowledged in feedback based on a prior output. If feedback is given with the due respect and recognition of an official's legitimacy, then the granting of authority is continued. If feedback is given with anger and resentment, or forms of rebellion and disruption, then authority could be eroding, and the process of maintaining authority is not being done well.

An evaluative study can also begin by selecting a particular function of the system – inputs, conversion, outputs, or feedback. The operational goodness of each function in the system can be assessed by the following four step method.

The Good Input Process

1) In making the determination that a set of social interactions can be classified as a "political system," minimal behavior constituting an input function will have been observed. Now, a fuller description of its operation is required prior to assessing the function's operational goodness. The roles and behavior of both authorities and political actors will be included in the description of the input process. The literature from explanatory political science can be used as a source of facts.

2) Based on the description of how it operates, an assessment can be made of the degree to which this input behavior fulfills the Flow Chart's standard of goodness for it. How well is this function performing? Does information flow smoothly through it? Are there stresses on the process causing snags, or disruptions? If so, what are they?

But such flow is not, in itself, an indicator of fairness or justice. An input process can flow as an operation, even if the masses are oppressed and their wants disregarded, provided they remain passive rather than rebel or otherwise interfere with the flow of the process. This is why a realistic assessment of the input function requires the third step – a look at the intrinsic dimension.

3) In the intrinsic dimension, the researcher asks, how do the members involved in, or excluded from, this input function feel about their experience with it? Are they supportive? For example, do all, some, or none of them feel that the input process is efficient, or fair, or easy to use? What percent of respondents, or interviewees, feel that the process is inefficient, or full of waste, fraud, and abuse, or is otherwise unjust, biased, etc.? Ideally, a function would elicit support, and not generate hostility. While no guarantee, fully supported functions can facilitate a system's persistence. Thus, to the extent that an input function sparks dissatisfaction, its rating will decrease. A system's full potential for operational goodness cannot be achieved while it engages in self-harming behavior.

Suppose there are laws suppressing some forms of speech, such as in Thailand, where a person can be put in prison for "insulting the king." Speech suppressing laws can restrict the free flow of the input that the members of a system might want to send to the conversion process. Likewise, allowing corporations unlimited independent expenditures in US campaigns gives them an input advantage over the common citizen who lacks the wealth of the superrich. Such speech favoritism could cause resentment or protest among the masses putting stress on the system, and thus reducing the goodness rating of the input function. But if the people do nothing, then the process can flow well.

If there are members of the system whose desire to make inputs is frustrated, what are the conditions of this situation? In other words, why do they feel this way? Such feelings among the members of a behavioral political system are a part of its political reality. So they are a necessary element in the evaluation of how well a given function in the system is operating.

4) As will be discussed in the Conclusion to this Chapter, a summary assessment of the goodness of the input process under study can be made by considering the findings in steps two and three together.[49]

The Good Conversion Process

1) As with the input function, a detailed description of how inputs are turned into outputs is necessary for evaluating a system's operational goodness. The processes of policy making and legislating are often extremely complex. An evaluative political scientist can draw from the existing explanatory literature to show how the function operates. Once the facts have been presented about how the conversion process works in a particular behavioral political system, then assessments of its operational goodness can be formulated and justified.

2) Easton's systems theory does not proscribe how the conversion process ought to be conducted in a behavioral political system. He understood that every system will have a unique set of behaviors for carrying out this function. Because every system will have a novel set of governing institutions, there is no one size fits all for this process.

However, since the process is a performance of converting inputs into outputs, there are some generally applicable operational standards. For example, upon describing the process, the political scientist can make estimates of its operational efficiency (the prudent use of resources) and efficacy (achieving its aims). Is there waste, fraud, and abuse? If so, these can be discussed. Are important matters handled expeditiously, or is there undue delay? Is the flow of the process hampered by corruption, dissension, or other interfering factors? Does the process earn supportive behavior from politically attentive members, or does it attract vocal criticism or active protest? If there are aggrieved or neglected members of the system, and they do nothing to disrupt the conversion process, then it will appear to be doing well operationally.

3) As to the intrinsic dimension, one indicator of the conversion function's operational goodness is how the political actors involved with it feel about it. For example, do all, some, or none of the legislators feel that the conversion process is efficient, or fair, or easy to use? The same can be asked of citizen petitioners, or of lobbyists. What percent of respondents, or interviewees, feel that the process is inefficient, or full of waste, fraud, and abuse; or is otherwise unjust, etc.? Why do they feel this way? For instance, are there people who petition the authorities to have inputs converted into outputs and are frustrated by the process? If so, what was their experience? Perhaps the process favors the few and frustrates the many. This is a rich area for detailed research.

4) As with inputs, a summary assessment of the goodness of the conversion process under study can be made by considering the findings in steps two and three together.

The Good Output Process

1) Having initially observed at least minimal behavior of an output function, a closer study can be made to assess its operational goodness. This will require, of course, an expanded description of how the function is performed.

2) Outputs are actions taken by authorities in the governing process. They are "the authoritative allocation of values." Broadly construed, the output process can include the implementation of law and policy, the administration of programs by agencies, and the judicial function of applying law to particular cases. The operational goodness of each of these complex governing functions in a behavioral political system can be measured.

There are several things to consider when assessing the operational goodness of the output process. These depend on what is factually happening in the particular political system under study. Is there waste, fraud, and abuse interfering with the flow of the operation? Another consideration is the responsiveness of the outputs to particular inputs. If the outputs are responses to prior demands, how responsive are they? To what degree do the outputs meet each item in the demands to which they are responses? Thus, one way the political scientist can assess the responsiveness of outputs is by comparing the product to the prior demand for it.

3) One consideration in the intrinsic dimension is as to how the outputs are received by the groups and individuals who have an interest in those productions. In other words, how satisfied with the outputs are the relevant parties? For example, how do small farmers feel about the new law granting corn subsidies, but terminating tobacco subsidies? Easton thoroughly examines how the effectiveness of outputs can be assessed by the kind and amount of support the recipients put back into the system. This could include the continued support for the function by a political party, special interests, or public interest groups. He also observes that "output failure" could result in a withdrawal of support, or a more hostile action, causing stress on the system.[50]

Another consideration is whether the outputs are being received as "authoritative" by the groups and individuals who have an interest in them. A crises of legitimacy could threaten the persistence of the system. Are there groups and individuals who feel neglected or unheard and therefore resentful toward the authorities? If outputs are causing stress among the membership, to what degree, if any, does this stress threaten the system? Outputs that generate so much frustration and resentment that the system is threatened can significantly detract from the function's operational goodness rating.

A behavioral political system courting self-destruction is clearly not functioning up to par. Thus, outputs are a key function for the persistence of a system in its environment.[51] Concerning the behavioral political system, Easton observes that "through its outputs it may find a way to persist in a potentially stressful environment."[52] Outputs, for example, can be used to appease the aggrieved, or to shore up support.

4) Like the other functions, a summary assessment of the goodness of the output process under study can be made by considering the findings in steps two and three together.

The Good Feedback Process

1) Having already observed at least minimal feedback behavior, a closer study can be made to assess its operational goodness. This will require, of course, an expanded description of how the function operates.

2) Feedback is generally communication from members to the authorities concerning actions they have taken in the governing process. It can take any or all of the forms that provide inputs into a system, such as emailing, contributing to election campaigns, etc. Unobstructed and freely flowing feedback can present an opportunity for the members to participate in the governing process, and an opportunity for the authorities to correct mistakes, to appease critics, or to defuse hostility in the system's membership. Supportive feedback is more likely to facilitate system persistence than negative feedback, unless the system can resolve the issues raised by the negative feedback.

3) When groups or individuals give feedback to the authorities, they of course want to be heard. To the extent they feel unheard, or heard and neglected or rejected, or the feedback process is constrained by oppressive laws, resentment may result. A system will do well to pay special attention to the attitudes of the politically relevant members, such as civic leaders, powerful lobbyists, public intellectuals, popular opinion makers, etc. An unresponsive political system could be acting against its own interest in self-preservation, or persistence, and is surely performing in a subpar manner. Marie Antoinette's reply, when told the

poor of Paris were starving, "let them eat cake," symbolizes a fatally wrong way to receive feedback. An inquiry into how members feel about the feedback process can reveal much about how well the system is performing.

4) Like the other functions, a summary assessment of the goodness of the feedback process under study can be made by considering the findings in steps two and three together. This will be discussed further in the Conclusion to this Chapter.

Synergy and the Quality of "Flow" as a Standard of Operational Goodness

When the performance of each function is analyzed in isolation from the other functions, the operation of the system as a whole is not considered. Estimating, or assessing, the general operational goodness of a political system will involve more than just adding up the sum of its parts. How the parts work together to generate a continuous flow of information throughout the system is a matter that *transcends* the mere examination of individual parts. Here, the quality of the flow is not a matter of the parallel operation of adjacent parts, but of the synergy created by all the parts working together.

Because such a rating cannot be reduced to an arithmetic calculation, this evaluation will require a degree of informed judgment, or connoisseurship, cultivated within the political science profession. Whether a system is awarded a Blue Ribbon, a Dunce Cap, or something in between, is an evaluation a political scientist can suggest in the conclusion of her or his study of the particular system's operational goodness. Indeed, such estimations will surely stimulate debate among the relevant experts within the profession. These disputes may reach consensus, even if not closure. This learning process will result in a refinement of understanding for political scientists, and may raise the quality of political science knowledge.

Yet there is still one other dimension of a behavioral political system to be assessed before a fully inclusive rating of the performance of the system can be given. That is the intrinsic dimension of the system *as a whole*. So far, the feelings of members have been discussed in relation to a specific function, input, output, etc. But there is a much broader dimension to political life – the way members experience it, and feel about life within their political system.

Assessing the Intrinsic Dimension of a Behavioral Political System

We have seen that, following Hartman's value science, there are three dimensions in which action is required to evaluate the goodness of a behavioral political system. In the systemic dimension the confirmation is made that the object of study qualifies as a "political system." In the extrinsic dimension the operational goodness of the system is assessed by comparing it to Easton's Flow Chart, which defines his concept of a "political system" and implies the standards for assessment. To complete the evaluation of the system as a whole requires an examination of the intrinsic dimension of the system. What that entails will now be explained.

From the point of view of evaluative political science, the intrinsic dimension of a behavioral political system consists of the feelings, as distinct from the behavior, of a system's membership. Not just any and all feelings are of interest. Instead, the focus encompasses what I will call the "politically relevant feelings." Without using the term "intrinsic dimension," Easton extensively discusses some of the politically relevant feelings of the membership of the behavioral political system. However, his focus is mainly on those positive and negative feelings related to "support." After a short summary of Easton's discussion of politically relevant feelings, I will show how that notion is expanded in the practice of evaluation.

Supportive Feelings as Potential

Supportive feelings can be expressed in such actions as voting for a party or candidate, volunteering for a campaign, or contributing to a party or a campaign. Writing letters, calling, emailing, or lobbying authorities are just a few of the many possible forms of support as an input into a system. As we have seen, for Easton support plays an important part in explaining how a particular behavioral political system manages to persist in its environment.

Easton notes that support can be "transactional." That is, groups of people can behave in supportive ways because the outputs they receive satisfy the demands they had put into the system. But support can also be "diffuse." That is, non-transactional support given out of such motivations as identifying oneself with the myths and symbols of one's country, e.g., patriotism.[53] The withdrawal of support by influential political elites, or a critical mass of the system's membership, can cause considerable stress for a system, threatening its persistence. Such withdrawal is often a part of the explanation of how a government falls out of power.

Members of a system can have supportive feelings without expressing them in overt behavior. Easton notes that covert supportive feelings are important for both political scientists and system authorities to understand because they have the *potential* to be called into action if needed.[54] While supportive behavior is vital to sustain political life, it need not be freely given. Supportive behavior can be compelled by an authoritarian government, such as the Dictator receiving over 90% of the vote in every "election." Presumably, some of these voters will have engaged in supportive behavior, but without actually feeling supportive of the Dictator. Thus, discerning whether political behavior is an accurate indicator of covert politically relevant feelings or not requires the cautious interpretation of a trained political scientist. Whether a system can persist for a longer time on voluntary support than it can on coerced support is an open question.

Contentment Index

Easton's concern with the intrinsic dimension of the behavioral political system was exclusively within the context of explanatory political science. Those feelings of the system's membership that are relevant to the persistence interest of the system define the intrinsic dimension for Easton. Indeed, he has proposed "an index of political contentment."[55] This index "would measure the probable degree of support" the members might give the system. Membership feeling could range from supportive, to indifference, to hostile. The latter feelings could be examined for their potential as a threat to a system. In other words, the index would provide a way to warn authorities about possible sources of stress, or threats to persistence. Like a thermometer, it could be used to test whether public hostility was nearing the boiling point. If that happens, then the authorities could produce outputs designed to raise the level of satisfaction, and put out the fire.

Satisfaction *As Such*

Understanding the feelings, meanings, or attitudes that give rise to either supportive or hostile behavior is one among many of the important elements of explanatory political science. However, for evaluative political science, the range of politically relevant feelings to be found in a behavioral political system is not one among many interests, it is *the primary* subject of research. Here the aim is not to explain system persistence, but to evaluate the intrinsic goodness of a system. Here, the focus is on feelings. This is a different point of view than the one with such concerns as gauging the security of a regime as implied by public contentment and of estimating the degree of potential threats to persistence.

The focus of study in the intrinsic dimension is on the membership's politically relevant feelings *as such*; that is, how the members feel about life in relation to their political system. This feeling is different than transactional satisfaction or dissatisfaction. It is also different than "diffuse" feelings reflecting loyalty to a nation's symbols.

To understand the quality of political life as that is experienced by the system's members is a distinct research project. Understanding that experience is more important for intrinsic evaluation than is the behavior of a system's membership. Instead, this evaluative effort is to take the measure of "political happiness" or "membership satisfaction." The higher these indicators are, the better is the political system. Ideally, the best political system would be the one in which the membership's full potential for satisfaction has been reached.

Easton uses the term "political contentment," but only as an item that indicates safety from the persistence point of view. A politically contented membership is unlikely to put stress on the system. But contentment need not be seen solely for its potential effect on persistence. Indeed, membership satisfaction can, and should, be understood as an element of political reality in itself, albeit with at least one qualification.

That is, whether for explanation or evaluation, history shows that, in the long run, all politically relevant feelings are, at least potentially, related to persistence. Down the road, politically relevant feelings can change, and the positive can become hostile, just as the negative can become supportive, and passivity become active. An assessment of intrinsic goodness is just a snapshot, a moment in time, and no guarantee of positive or negative feelings in the future. Thus, in the explanatory approach, persistence is proximal, but within the evaluative interpretive framework persistence is distal, yet not entirely out of the picture.

Suppose, for example, that substantial sectors of the membership feel alienated from the centers of power, inefficacious, or neglected by their authorities but remain politically passive. In this context, they would not constitute an immediate threat to the system's persistence. An explanation of how the system persists would describe how the political functions are carried out, but need not dwell on the compliant masses. Indeed, the functions of a system could be carried out with efficiency and effectiveness, measuring high in operational goodness, even while the masses lived in alienation and fear, provided they did not act to disrupt the flow of the system. Their passivity would render them unimportant from both the persistence perspective and for the project of measuring the system's operational goodness in the extrinsic dimension.

However, while virtually invisible extrinsically, unhappy feelings would have a significant impact on the measure of the intrinsic goodness of a system despite the passivity of their behavior. With a major part of the membership feeling such passive hostility, the behavioral political system under study, while temporarily safe, would be assessed by evaluative political science as far from its full potential for intrinsic goodness.

The Operation/Feeling Relationship

Once the extent of political happiness *in general* has been found out, the results of the research can be published. This opens the way to further research challenges. For example, why do these folks feel this way? Is there any non-transactional relationship between the operation of the system and the feelings of its members? This line of questioning hints at the possibility of a multifaceted complex causal relationship existing between the politically relevant feelings of the members of a political system and the operations of the system. How does life in this system result in the degree of political happiness discovered by research? In other words, once the facts of their feelings have been determined, diagnosing the causes of a people's political happiness or unhappiness is a second research challenge. Thus, evaluative political science broadens the area of public opinion research to include the Index of Contentment that Easton envisioned.

A Positivist Argument

A positivist might argue that while operational goodness may be measurable, membership sentience is irrelevant to the goodness of a political system. In this view, operational flow is the sole standard. If many members are miserable and suffering, it does not matter provided the system is working well. This could be an argument, for example, in favor of the Antebellum South. The system is working well, they would say, and the political elites and slave owners see nothing wrong and want to keep the system as it is. But in that view, the political reality of membership feeling would have to be ignored. However, if political science is to be true to its name, then a major portion of the political system, the reality of human feeling, cannot be disregarded. For long periods in the Antebellum South, the absence of overt protest or rebellion did not imply bliss consciousness among the enslaved; even though their oppressors may have made that claim.

In this case, the suffering was endured without being potential political behavior. The feelings of helplessness kept their pain "politically irrelevant" for the ruling class. But in the view of evaluative political science, such suffering is central to the intrinsic measure of the behavioral political system's goodness. So despite the fact that the masses are passive, the more unhappiness they feel, the lower the system's rating on intrinsic goodness.

Criteria

For the purpose of establishing criteria for rating the intrinsic goodness of a political system, and for ranking it in comparison with others, an intrinsically good political system can be defined as one which embraces a politically satisfied membership. The facts about how folks feel determine the assessment of intrinsic goodness made by the political scientist. Membership satisfaction, then, is the determining norm for assessing the intrinsic goodness of a behavioral political system. Again, in this analysis, the likely consequences for persistence need not be considered.

Someone might ask why that standard is used, and not another. Easton notes that culture can set up expectations of the political system.[56] Different cultures might have different standards for intrinsic goodness. One might ask, then, whether this "membership satisfaction" standard is a product of Western hedonistic culture. Perhaps there is some other standard by which to assess a system's intrinsic goodness.

However, there is evidence in history that political discontent can be an experienced feeling across cultures. Many revolutions over time and around the world have been based on the belief that a better, or more satisfying, political life would be possible if the current government is ousted. Clearly, membership satisfaction, or dissatisfaction, is a cross-cultural phenomenon.

Even without reference to the past, empathy and compassion seem to compel the principle that the number of members feeling satisfied and the saliency of their satisfaction are the proper data points to be sought for evaluating the intrinsic goodness of a behavioral political system. Upon those facts an assessment can be made.

Intuitively it seems that few people could seriously contend that a life of political alienation and misery is better than a life in which the membership of a political system are genuinely satisfied. Of course, the professional political scientist will be trained to discern the genuine expression of feelings among a public from the fearful or inauthentic expression of feelings. Therefore, using the concept of "authentic membership satisfaction" as the measure seems to be the best possible method for political scientists to rate a behavioral political system's intrinsic goodness.[57] Such feelings are an element of political knowledge in the Normative Political Science paradigm. The methodology for assessing membership satisfaction in China's political system will be discussed in the next chapter.

Legitimacy

Another indicator of membership satisfaction can be the degree to which the authorities are acknowledged as legitimate by the members of the system. Public opinion studies can reveal this attitude. Also, defiance of laws can be interpreted as a form of political rebellion. Whether robbing banks or running stop signs, violations of the law imply a lack of respect for the laws broken, and perhaps a degree of disrespect for the law makers. Such behavior can be interpreted for its implications of civic discontent, which can be expressed in many forms.

Likewise, when members of a system regularly obey it's laws, and do so with little or no government compulsion, then an interpreter will likely find that this behavior is an expression of political contentment. Of course, each behavioral political system is unique, and the feelings of the people will be related to the context in which they are living. So when grand generalizations about the meaning of political behavior are made without reference to facts in context, a scientist should treat them with skepticism. Also, as with any complex society, and as The Law of Scarcity predicts, even people living in heterogeneous societies invariably have competing and conflicting interests, so the chance of ever seeing a score of perfect political contentment for any political system is probably low.[58]

Methods

Feelings about the quality of political life have been studied on a regular basis in traditional opinion surveys. For example, some surveys instruct respondents to "indicate on a scale of 1 to 10, how strongly you agree with the statement that 'my government cares about people like me.'" There are a variety of methods for finding out how the members feel about life in relation to their political system. Interpretive mixed methods, still being refined, can be much more sensitive to politically relevant feelings than large surveys.[59] Participant observation, ethnography, focus groups, and individual interviews have been shown to be very revealing by the interpretive political scientists who are skilled at using them. But if the existing political science literature is found to be inadequate or incomplete, then research from other fields can be consulted. Social psychology and sociology, for instance, have vast quantities of research which may help in understanding and gauging the satisfaction of the membership in a system. Of course, new studies can and will be done by evaluative political scientists as they research, rate, and rank various political systems.

Empathy is the essential method for acquiring data about the intrinsic dimension of a political system. Using empathy as a method, the political scientist relates to the subject matter person-to-person, more at the level of sentience than intellect. Even in the intellectual preparation of a large survey, formulating the questions to be asked requires the scientist to enter into a personal relationship with the imagined respondents. Empathy is necessary for interpreting survey results as well. In a trained and skillful interpreter, empathic methods can be a fruitful way to acquire the data about a population which is necessary to evaluate a system's intrinsic goodness.[60]

Authenticity

Exercising empathy should also entail the skill in a political scientist at detecting inauthentic expressions of political contentment. This skill is crucial to constructing a professionally meaningful rating of membership satisfaction. For instance, in oppressive political systems respondents might give "safe" answers to questions about their feelings rather than report authentic expressions of their true views. Also, public sentience can be manipulated by deceitful or clever means, such as the Roman gimmick of "bread and circuses." An example of another trick is the use of the drug "soma" in Aldous Huxley's novel, *Brave New World*.[61] The members of a behavioral political system may be too fearful to express their true feelings, or they might not be aware of what their true feelings are. The interpretive political scientist may be able to use his or her skills and abilities to empathically discern what folks actually feel even if they misrepresent their feelings, are afraid to express their feelings, or lack the self-awareness required to know how they feel. Thus, in an assessment of a system's intrinsic goodness, the way the authenticity issue was dealt with may have to be discussed and its impact on the evaluation considered.[62]

Whether eliciting voluntary support with bribes or gimmicks, or commanding support with the threat of punishment, from the persistence point of view, any support will do. But for the political scientist's purpose of assessing the system's intrinsic goodness, the generation of inauthentic, or artificial, support would be treated as a "Potemkin Village," and an understanding of the true feelings of the people would be sought.[63]

Irrelevant Feelings

As we have seen, for evaluative political science, politically relevant feelings include those sentiments related to a person's quality of life in a behavioral political system. Another task for the political scientist, then, is to sort out politically *irrelevant* feelings. These could include, for example, what Henry David Thoreau calls "lives of quiet desperation," or the suffering of existential angst and ennui, psychological problems, unhappy family life, or bothersome religious uncertainties. Such feelings could color responses to questions about the quality of life in a political system. A skillful interpretivist will be able to sort out a mix of emotions, and identify the politically related sentiments. Of course, any of these feelings could become politically related if people blame the government for them, or if the people demand that the government fix their unhappiness, or fill their empty lives.

Conclusion: Questions for Further Research and the Prospects for Political Science

A Quantitative Gauge of Feelings?

As I mentioned earlier, Easton has proposed constructing "an index of political contentment." He thought that, like a thermometer, it could be used to test whether public hostility was nearing the boiling point. If that happens, then the authorities could produce outputs designed to reduce the threat.

One problem with this idea, which Easton also noted, is that currently the ranking of politically relevant feelings, such as those from supportive to hostile, can only be done qualitatively and not with the quantitative precision of a thermometer.[64] The same challenge exists for evaluative political science. Like pain and pleasure, general intrinsic goodness can be ranked qualitatively to reflect its intensity. For example, from low, to medium, to high; or, even from 1 to 10. But the metrics for membership satisfaction are currently nowhere as precise as are, for example, those for air temperature.[65]

Can the measure of a system's intrinsic goodness ever be quantified? Perhaps. It may be possible that after extensive studies in a variety of political systems and their cultures, a strong consensus of political scientists could agree on some kind of numerical system to add a finer grade of precision to such terms as support, hostility, and membership satisfaction.[66]

The Total Goodness Measure

At least in principle, once the general level of membership satisfaction has been determined, then it can be considered along with the evaluation of a system's operational goodness to characterize the system's overall goodness – *the Total Goodness Measure.* However, as we have seen, measuring intrinsic goodness differs from the measurement of operational goodness. And the subject matter for both are different in kind – operation and feeling. So, if there are two different metrics, one for operational goodness, and one for intrinsic goodness, and these refer to two different subjects, then maybe the final evaluation can only be expressed in these two ratings; operational goodness and intrinsic goodness. In the alternative, the political scientist can offer a professional opinion as to the total goodness of a political system, based on its operational and intrinsic goodness. Such an opinion can also be offered in the fourth step for assessing the overall goodness of each function in a political system, as discussed earlier in this Chapter.

At first, it may seem that the quantification of operational goodness appears an easier task than that of intrinsic goodness. Performance specifications for functions can be quantified, and fulfillment can be measured. But, as Easton asked, how can the support or hostility for a particular function be quantified?[67] Also, to measure *synergy* requires that the whole system be seen as more than the sum of its parts; a vision that positivists would likely deny is possible.

Presently, then, evaluative political science can show the way to assess the goodness of a behavioral political system using such qualitative terms as excellent, medium, and poor, for a particular system, and better/best, or worse/worst for comparing systems. While this is a giant step forward for political science, the problem of quantification remains a challenge.

The End of Political Philosophy?

As we have seen, the "norm" for Normative Political Science is Easton's conception of the political system. As a norm, it has two primary functions. One is that it can organize and guide empirical research so as to stay within the realm of the field and create a body of political science knowledge. The other function, as shown here, is that it can serve as a standard by which to evaluate the goodness of a behavioral political system. As we have seen, the Total Goodness of a political system depends on how well a system satisfies a) the definition for it, and b) the people in it. These measurements are not dependent upon the political philosophy of the political scientist. As with taking air temperature, a libertarian and an authoritarian can reach the same results when assessing goodness, because the assessment depends entirely on the facts of the situation.

In Normative Political Science, membership satisfaction research is the ultimate political science test of a behavioral political system's goodness. From this point of view, how folks feel in a system is more important than how well the system operates. If an operationally inept system embraces widespread authentic contentment, then the final judgment of it must be that it is a good political system. If a system is operationally sharp as a tack, but most members are miserable in it, then it must be judged as a poor political system. Thus, Normative Political Science lets the authentic feelings of the people be the final judge of their political system's goodness. This interpretive framework, then, liberates the political science profession from both the positivist's denial that the goodness of a political system can be rationally appraised, and from the centuries old disputations over what standards to use in such an appraisal.

Philosophical notions like "democracy," "socialism," "communism," "justice," "equality," "freedom," or "liberty" lack precise definitions and clear examples in reality. They are emotionally laden terms used by political actors to stimulate membership behavior in the *practice* of politics within a system. Just as Easton noted, forms of government and philosophical ideals are not the focus of interest for his explanatory political science (as discussed in the above subsection, "Flow and the Form of Government"), so they are not relevant to the evaluative political science assessment of a system's goodness. As Supreme Court Justice, Oliver Wendel Holmes, understood, there is no Universal Standard of Justice looming over the world, "like a brooding omnipresence in the sky."[68] I would add that, given the absence of such standard, to know when a political system is good, there is only the fact-based professionally evaluated goodness of a particular behavioral political system.[69]

A New Task for Comparative Political Science

Evaluative political science can rate the operational and intrinsic goodness of a political system, and then rank systems according to their comparative goodness. As pure research, this is a descriptive process, and not prescriptive. Once the evaluative process for a behavioral political system has been completed, problems will become apparent for which applied political scientists can trace their causes, and perhaps suggest ways to improve a system's ranking.

Over time, the American Political Science Association could establish a role for itself in the USA, and around the world, like that of The National Institute of Health and The World Health Organization. In other words, the political science profession could make of itself a source of information for humanity about both the goodness of political systems and the ways of making them better, just as the NIH and WHO are sources for everyone about matters of public health. To achieve this status we political scientists need only commit to the standards and methods of Normative Political

Science. In Chapter Five we will show how the American political science profession can be re-organized to facilitate the actual practice of Normative Political Science, and thereby cultivate for itself a new image in our society, and around the world, as a source of political wisdom.

But before that, in the next chapter, Chapter 4, we will apply the principles of evaluative political science to the nation of China. We will inquire as to the operational goodness of the Chinese political system, and as to the political happiness of its members. The results may surprise some readers.

Endnotes

[1] Although contemporaries, the two men probably never met, and their writings were probably unknown to each other.

[2] Hartman, 1967.

[3] Easton's political theory, particularly his idea of "persistence," is strongly influenced by his understanding of the biology of his time. But exactly what strand of biology has influenced him is not entirely clear. Nor is it clear how far he would take the analogy.

In my view, the phrase "the struggle for persistence" can be used to explain the operation of the political system. That is a take on the Darwinian notion of "the struggle for survival." But can this transference of Darwinian notions to Easton's political theory be extended to say that political systems exemplify "the survival of the fittest," or "only the strongest political systems survive"? The second phrase seems beyond the pale to me. Darwin was no "Social Darwinist," and neither was Easton.

Easton would likely agree, in my opinion, with the notion that those political systems which persist are the ones which, among other things, most accurately perceive their environment and successfully adapt to it. In this sense, a kind of political intelligence can be attributed to persisting systems. However, the term "adaptation" can imply a passivity that could mislead a researcher when trying to understand the success of a political system at persistence. Political intelligence can also include foresight, sensitivity to public sentiments, awareness of threats from within and from outside the system. In addition, ingenuity and energetic action can play important parts for explaining persistence. The ability of elites to develop unity with the masses may be a factor. (China, as discussed in Chapter Four, could be an example of that.) The role of good and bad fortune must also be considered. Chance surely plays a significant role in persistence. So no easy generalization is likely to explain all cases of political system persistence. The Aristotelian Forms of Government seem to me to be irrelevant philosophical notions devoid of explanatory usefulness.

[4] For a discussion of Easton as an interpretivist, and why he is not a positivist, see Kelleher, William. 2017. Letting Easton be Easton—an Interpretivist. Qualitative & Multi-Method Research. 15(2): 22-28. DOI 10.31235/osf.io/cmnvx Entire Issue,
https://www.maxwell.syr.edu/uploadedFiles/moynihan/cqrm/qmmr_files/QMMR15_2.pdf
Single essay, https://osf.io/preprints/socarxiv/cmnvx/
As John Gunnell has observed, and which is discussed in the QMMR paper, the association of Easton with positivistic behavioralism has been a reification of ignorance and misunderstanding in the political science profession since the 1960s.

[5] To adapt Hartman's value science to Easton's political science, I will discuss the systemic dimension as the conceptual element of evaluation. The extrinsic dimension will be discussed as the operational element. The intrinsic dimension consists of the intentional, or mental, realm of feelings, attitudes, and meanings.

[6] See note 4, above.

[7] A Framework for Political Analysis (herein after "Easton 1965 a"), page 96.

[8] Ibid., 50.

[9] See Diagram 3, the simplified flow chart, 1965 a, 112. Also, Diagram 2, A Systems Analysis of Political Life (herein after "Easton 1965 b"), 32.

[10] Hartman uses the term "value" in the sense of the general concept. Easton uses the term in the sense of particular values.

[11] RE complex models, see 1965 a, 110, and 1965 b, 30.

[12] Easton 1965 b, 29.

[13] Ibid., 29.

[14] Ibid., 479.

[15] Ibid., 29.

[16] Chapter Five will discuss Easton's reforms for the organization of the political science profession.

[17] Easton 1965 a, 112.

[18] Ibid., 75.

[19] Ibid., 86. Cf. n. 3, above.

[20] Ibid., 109.

[21.] Easton 1965 b, 31. Persistence is not the same as "equilibrium." Easton rejects the equilibrium metaphor, because, among other things, it implies stasis as an ideal when the political system is dynamic. Also the equilibrium model characterizes the political process in mechanical terms when, in Easton's view, the behavior of political actors is primarily based on their own agency and decision making, and is not a mechanical tendency. Equilibrium is discussed further in Chapter One.

[22.] Easton 1965 b, 475, Easton 1965 a, 79.

[23.] Easton 1965 a, 55, 71, cf. Easton 1965 b, 479.

[24.] Easton 1965 b, 478.

[25.] Easton 1965 a, 79, cf. Easton 1965b, 78. Easton's rejection of the "state," and other proposed defining concepts for political science, are discussed in Kelleher 2017, Back to the Future.

[26.] Easton 1965 a, 53.

[27.] Ibid., 53 Another way to say this is to use Lasswell's famous language; that is, the authoritative allocation of values settles conflicts over who get what, when, and how. AF 96 But Easton distinguishes his theory from that of Lasswell, see note 4, above.

[28.] Easton 1965 b, 53.

[29.] Ibid., 55.

[30.] Ibid., 55.

[31.] Ibid., 90.

[32.] Ibid., 91.

[33.] Ibid., 80.

[34.] Ibid., 26.

[35.] Ibid., 26.

[36.] Ibid., 26.

[37.] Ibid., 26.

[38.] Ibid., 7.

[39.] Easton 1965 b, 479, cf. 1965 a, 29f.

[40.] Easton 1965 a, 97.

[41.] Ibid., 97.

[42.] Ibid., 97.

[43.] Ibid., 97.

[44.] See Easton's discussion of "parapolitical systems," Ibid., 52f.

[45.] Ibid., 82.

[46.] Ibid., 80.

[47.] For instance, Easton discusses the rise of industrialization out of feudalism. The input/output processes persisted even as major changes took place in the political institutions. See Easton 1965 b, 154f.

[48] In note 3, above, some similarities of Darwin's theory of evolution and Easton's theory of the political system were considered. Easton's vision of the political system unfolding over time also has some similarities reminiscent of Henri Bergson's 1907 book, Creative Evolution.

[49] As stated above, the problems of gauging an over-all performance rating will be discussed further towards the end of this chapter.

[50] See Easton 1965 b, 230 passim.

[51] For political science, to be "authoritative" the outputs must be the products of authorities. Identifying who the authorities are in a particular behavioral political system is a matter for empirical study. Because political science is the study of behavior in relation to the authoritative allocation of values for society as a whole, other forms by which values are allocated are not central to the professional concerns of political scientists. For example, the Academy of Motion Picture Arts and Sciences awards Oscars to folks in the movie business. This authoritative allocation of values, in itself, is not political. Of course, the Academy, actors, producers, and all sorts of other workers in the movie business can engage in political activity after the awards are given. Charities allocate values to the needy. University Admissions Departments allocate values to the applicants who hope they can study there. As such, these are usually not political activities because they are not based on policies meant for the society *as a whole*.

If allocations of value are only for some special interests, and not society as a whole, then the system's operational goodness may be diminished accordingly. Suppose that, in the USA, Republicans say their tax cuts for the wealthy are good for the whole society due to "trickle down" benefits, such as job hiring or increased wages. If this proves untrue, then, by definition, the Republicans have diminished the operational goodness of the political system by their selfishness.

[52] Easton 1965 b, 477.

[53] While Easton discusses the importance of support, both specific and diffuse, throughout his writings, Chapters 10 and 17, in 1965 b, are especially rich. However, for evaluative political science, support per se is only one indicator of a system's intrinsic goodness. In taking this measure, a variety of interpretive methods inquiring into the politically relevant feelings of the membership is necessary.

[54] See Easton's discussion of overt and covert support at 1965 b, 159f.

[55] Ibid., 405-406.

[56] Ibid., 404f.

[57] The Utilitarianism of such philosophers as Jeremy Bentham, advocates the principle of "the greatest good for the greatest number." But the Utilitarian principle is inconsistent with Normative Political Science on at least two counts.

First, Utilitarianism neither focuses on the functioning of the political system, nor has a way of taking the measure of its operational goodness. Secondly, the objectivist bias in Utilitarianism precludes the consideration of the feelings of a system's membership, and makes the philosopher the sole judge as to whether "the greatest number" is receiving "the greatest good."

[58.] See Easton's discussions of scarcity, notes 25-29, above.

[59.] Few scholars have done as much to bring together, to refine, and to teach about interpretive methods for political science than Dvora Yanow and Peregrine Schwartz-Shea. For example, see the comprehensive study they have edited, including essays they have written – *Interpretation and Method Empirical Research Methods and the Interpretive Turn.* 2nd Edition. 2014. M. E. Sharpe, NY.

[60.] An excellent explanation of the role of intersubjective agreement in the process of validating interpretive science studies is given by Peregrine Schwartz-Shea in "Judging Quality Evaluative Criteria and Epistemic Communities," Chapter Seven, 120-146, *Interpretation and Method*, note 59 supra.

[61.] Chatto & Windus, London. 1932.

[62.] A study of Chinese political opinion attempted to assure authenticity by sending Chinese students, who could speak the local dialects, with a questionnaire and script to interview randomly selected people. Presumably, the students would present a non-threatening demeanor, and thus elicit authentic responses. See "The Zang Study" in Chapter Four.

[63.] Clearly, open societies are the best condition for the political science profession to do its work. To this end, the American Political Science Association can advocate for open societies so that members can do their work. Perhaps closed and dangerous societies can be named and shamed by the APSA.

[64.] Easton saw the difficulties of trying to quantify such politically relevant feelings as support, hostility, etc. Indeed, he declined to engage "the onerous and complex technical aspects involved" in the project. Easton 1965 b, 162. Yet he returned to the confounding conundrum in his discussion of ordinal and cardinal terms at Easton 1965 b, 161-165, and 168-170.

[65.] Prior to the 1700s there was no universally agreed upon way to measure temperature. Only different opinions. Then Fahrenheit and Celsius invented competing measures. Complete intersubjective agreement has still not been achieved, as the split between Europe and the USA over Fahrenheit and Celsius shows. See Chang, Hasok. Inventing Temperature: Measurement and Scientific Progress. Oxford University Press, USA. 2004.

[66.] On the general necessity for intersubjective agreement, and its role in the creation of quantification schemes, see the incisive essay by Dvora Yanow, "Neither Rigorous nor Objective? Interrogating Criteria for knowledge Claims in

Interpretive Science," Chapter Six, pages 97-119, Interpretation and methods, note 59 supra.

[67.] Incidentally, Easton commented that "it is impossible to speak meaningfully of support for a system as a whole [because that] is too undifferentiated an idea." Easton 1965 b, 165. However, he did have a sense that the membership can have a feeling about the system as a whole. He observed that "Environmental disturbances may help to shape not only what the members want, but *the sentiments* they display toward the political system *as a whole*, its institutions and leaders." Easton 1965b, 155 (it. ad.). He also noted that among the members there could be variations in "the level of satisfaction with experienced conditions." Easton 1965 b, 402.

[68.] Oliver Wendell Holmes wrote in a dissenting opinion in Southern Pacific Company v. Jensen, 244 U.S. 205, 222 (1917) that "[t]he common law is not a brooding omnipresence in the sky, but the articulate voice of some sovereign or quasi sovereign that can be identified."

[69.] In Chapter Five we will discuss Easton's vision of the place for applied political science, political philosophy, public intellectuals, and the role of the profession in politics.

Chapter Four:

Assessing the Goodness of a Political System with Chinese Characteristics

Introduction

We have said that the Normative Political Science paradigm is based on the Easton-Hartman Synthesis. That is, Easton's definition of the "political system," made to guide political science empirical research, is given the additional function of guiding the assessment of how well a particular political system is working. As will be discussed further in this Chapter's Conclusion, the use of this approach will help to pin point the location of dysfunction, and hence focus on the diagnosis of the causes of below par operations. Once these causes have been identified by political scientists, they can recommend remedies for them.

In this chapter we will illustrate the application of the Normative Political Science interpretive framework to the assessment of how well the political system of China operates. As we have seen, following Easton, the defining function of every political system is its effort at the authoritative allocation of values for a society. This process forms a system of five elements. These are, inputs, conversion, outputs, feedback, and the environment in which a particular system operates.[1] In political science, "goodness" need not be the stuff of political sentiments, such as the love of democracy and the hate of tyranny. Instead, as Hartman teaches, it can be an entirely fact-based assessment. Hartman also points out that goodness can be assessed in three different dimensions. These are the systemic, the extrinsic, and the intrinsic.[2] These concepts may seem rather airy without showing them in connection with something real on the ground. Hence, we will turn to China, less as a definitive analysis of the Chinese political system than as an illustration of this new method of analysis.

Does China have a Political System?

As Chapter Three showed (page 88f), the first step for an evaluative political science analysis is to be sure the political behavior under study constitutes a "political system." Of course, anyone can intuitively acknowledge that such a thing as a political system with Chinese characteristics exists. Sources attesting to that are abundant, from TV news and special programs, to newspapers, magazines, social media, etc. But a political science assessment of the goodness of China's political system requires more than an intuitive recognition. At least the basic elements of the system must be described so that we know the facts that will determine the measure of the system. Thus, in this chapter I will do three things. First, I will summarize the primary constituent elements of China's political system. Second, I will assess how well the system is operating. Third, I will discuss how the people in China feel about life in their political system. These endeavors correspond to Hartman's notions of the systemic, the extrinsic, and the intrinsic dimensions of evaluation.

Power in China's political system is organized in its regime. As Easton noted, a "regime" consists of a set of institutions, rules, and beliefs by which a political system is governed, and through which it operates to authoritatively allocate values.[3] China's regime has two primary sections, each with its own written constitution. These are the People's Republic of China (PRC) and the Chinese Communist Party (CCP). Because of this dual nature of the Chinese regime, it is often referred to as China's "Party-State." Our first challenge, then, is to find and describe those patterns of behavior in the Party-State that meet the five elements of Easton's definition of a political system.

Part One: The Systemic Dimension

As one might expect, because the population to be governed exceeds 1.4 billion people, the offices and officers that are active in governing are very numerous. A description of, and explanation about, these factors can become quite complex and detailed. Since the purpose of this chapter is merely to illustrate how an assessment of the system's goodness can be approached, only those institutions that are key from the political science point of view will be mentioned. These are the offices most directly related to the input-output function of the system. The many other offices are generally supplemental to those primary offices.

A. Introduction to the PRC Constitution

After the 1949 Revolution, Mao Zedong and the CCP declared the existence of the People's Republic of China (PRC). However, a formal constitution was not enacted until 1954. Since then, several changes have been made as part of leadership's learning process. In 1982 a revised Constitution was enacted, and it has subsequently been amended several times. The following discussion draws from the latest version of the PRC constitution.[4]

The National People's Congress

The PRC constitution establishes the National People's Congress (NPC) as the main legislative body of the regime (Articles 2 and 57). The NPC meets only once a year, typically in March, and usually for less than two weeks. It has about 3000 deputies, or delegates. Some of them are appointed, some elected by official bodies in the 24 provinces and numerous other districts in China. The NPC's term is for five years. For example, the 13th NPC's term began in March of 2018, and expired in March 2023. The 14th NPC will be in service from 2023 to 2028.[5]

During the NPC's short annual sessions, proposed legislation is usually introduced either by its members, or by its Standing Committee (more on that below). NPC sub-committees with area expertise meet and discuss the proposals relative to their jurisdiction. Later, the entire NPC votes to ratify particular proposals, which can include new laws, revisions of existing laws, or amendments to the PRC constitution. A two-thirds vote is required for constitutional amendments. A majority of votes is required to pass a law. That vote makes a law official. While the US constitution requires the president to sign a law to make it official, this is not required in China.

NPC Powers

Some of the other responsibilities of the NPC include electing the president and the vice president of the People's Republic of China, and the heads of the numerous other ministries, departments, and agencies. It also has the power of removal for these offices. One of the major responsibilities of the PNC is to oversee the nation's economic plans. These plans are often set to continue for five years. There are also five year plans for social development, including education, health care, etc. The five year plans are formulated after considerable consultation with the relevant government offices, the CCP, and sometimes private sector experts. The NPC is charged with approving the plans and the state budget.

One source of its power is that the NPC is given the task to independently audit all of the bureaucracy's expenditures of public funds. (Article 91) As China's military is under civilian control, the NPC is empowered to vote on military matters, including war and peace. (Although China has not had any wars since 1979, when it had a brief border dispute with Viet Nam.)

National People's Congress Standing Committee

One of the first orders of business for a new NPC is to elect its Standing Committee from among its members, which is done by majority vote. Like the NPC, it has a five year term. But, unlike the larger NPC, the Standing Committee is in session year around. It can exercise all the powers that the NPC has during its short session. (Articles 57, 58) The Standing Committee usually meets monthly or by-monthly. But it may also convene special sessions as needed. Currently at 175 members, the NPC Standing Committee enacts the vast majority of China's national laws and routinely conducts oversight of other governmental bodies. Standing Committee members are not allowed to simultaneously hold positions in executive, judicial, prosecutorial or supervisory posts. A Council of Chairpersons supervises the day-to-day work of the NPC's Standing Committee.

During the NPC's short session, the Standing Committee must report on all of its operations in the past year. While the NPC theoretically has oversight power, it generally does not contest Standing Committee operations. Also, when the Standing Committee submits bills for the NPC to enact, they are almost always approved with little dissent. In part, the lack of dissent is due to the Chinese custom of seeking consensus during the legislative process. Most bills go through a lengthy process of discussion by their sponsors with all the relevant members of the NPC sub-committees, and with the government bureaucracy.[6] Because it does not act alone, but through a consultative process, in my view, it is not correct to assume that the Standing Committee has, or exercises, dictatorial power in the legislative process.

The PRC Presidency

The PRC President is elected by the National People's Congress. (Article 79) In theory, any PRC citizen, who is at least 45 years old, can become president of the PRC, but no women have as yet. The term is five years. Mr. Xi Jinping is the current president. He first took office in March 2013. In March 2018 the two term limit on the presidency was lifted. In March of 2023 Mr. Xi was elected for a third term as president of the PRC. Whether or not Xi Jinping will be, or wants to be, president for a fourth term, or for life, remains to be seen.

The PRC presidency is a largely ceremonial office rather than an administrative post. He may host, for example, receptions related to foreign affairs and diplomacy. He may engage in publicity events, like the opening of new construction projects, factories, etc. The NPC and the Standing Committee can delegate some of their powers to the presidency, in which case he can sign presidential orders to exercise that power. Another source of power the presidency has is the responsibility to nominate the heads of the bureaucracy, which the NPC votes to approve or not. The president generally does not take executive action on his own prerogative, but acts under the guidance of the NPC, especially its Standing Committee.

The State Council

In the United States, the Cabinet consists of the heads of the various branches of the federal bureaucracy. The US president presides over the Cabinet. But in the PRC, bureaucratic departments, ministries, and agencies are in a separate organization called the "State Council." It is managed by the Premier of the State Council, not the PRC president. Thus, the State Council is the administrative branch of government (Article 85). It is primarily concerned with implementing the legislative outputs of the NPC and the Standing Committee. It is required to report on all of its affairs to the NPC during the annual session. The operations of the State Council are overseen by its Premier, currently Mr. Li Qiang. He was appointed to office on March 11, 2023, succeeding Mr. Li Keqiang.

The State Council has 35 members, including the premier, and four vice premiers, one of whom is a woman, Sun Chunlan. Ms. Sun is the highest placed woman in the PRC.[7] The other members include the heads of the ministries and agencies which do the actual day-to-day governing of China, such as agriculture, business, economic development, education, etc.

As part of its consultative process, the State Council often publicizes proposed actions, giving the public, and members of the government, time to comment, or give input.[8] Much of the feedback that goes into the political system will be based on the job performance of the various parts of the State Council bureaucracy.

B. The Second Constitution for the Chinese Political System

After stating that "the socialist system" is the PRC's "fundamental system," PRC constitution Article 1 then declares, "Leadership by the Communist Party of China is the defining feature of socialism with Chinese characteristics."[9] This statement makes the CCP the leading institution for China as a matter of Constitutional Law. The Party has its own constitution, which establishes its power hierarchy, and its rules for membership and operations.[10]

The CCP constitution states, "The highest leading bodies of the Party are the National Congress and the Central Committee which it elects." (Article 10) However, Article 10 does not accurately reflect the Party's locus of power in actual practice, as I will explain momentarily.

The National Congress

The National Congress meets every five years, but only for about a week to 10 days. It consists of delegates from all parts of the Communist Party, who are elected by members of the various Party organizations, such as those at the local and provincial levels. (Article 19) In October 2022, the CCP's 20th National Congress was held in the Great Hall of the People, in Beijing. About 2,300 delegates attended. They represented the estimated 90 million plus members of the Party.[11]

The agenda is prepared long in advance by members of the Central Committee, after consultations with all levels of the Party throughout the country. Among the responsibilities of the National Congress are to elect the members of the new Central Committee, and the Central Commission for Discipline Inspection, hear the reports of the prior Central Committee, take disciplinary action against members, if necessary, and discuss and make decisions on major issues concerning the Party. (Article 20)

The Central Committee

The Central Committee of the Party is elected for a term of five years. Aside from the National Congress, the Central Committee holds its own annual meetings just for its members, which number around 300. (Article 22) At these "plenary sessions," among other business, elections are held for the very top leadership. This includes the Political Bureau, currently with 25 members, and its Standing Committee, which currently has 7 members. The General Secretary, who is mainly the operational officer of the Central Committee, is selected from among the members of the Political Bureau's Standing Committee. (Article 23) While Article 10 appears to place the National Congress in an equal, or even superior, position to "the Central Committee which it elects," in practice, the officials elected during the plenary sessions are the primary locus of power in the CCP. Their order of importance can be seen in Article 23, which states that the 7 member Standing Committee has supervisorial power over the Political Bureau, which has supervisorial power over the Central Committee.[12]

However, the practice of regular consultations throughout the regime, and with the public, keep the policy-making process far from being solely top-down and dictatorial. Article 3 states that, to help build and preserve the Party, members should "maintain close ties with the people, share the ideas of the Party with them, consult with them as issues arise, keep the Party up to date on their views and demands, and defend their legitimate interests." (Unfortunately, writers on Chinese politics with a Western bias often fail to clarify how Article 3 consultations mix the locus of power in the governing process.)

Any Chinese person, at least 18 years old, who is willing to work for the Party, and pay its membership dues, can join the CCP. (Article 1) Members of the CCP are to be "vanguard fighters of the Chinese working class who possess Communist consciousness." (Article 2) "Party building" is something every member is urged to think about and to share ideas about with other members. They should "regularly discuss and examine the Party's promotional, educational, and organizational work, discipline inspection, its work with the people, and its work related to the united front; and carefully study current thinking and political trends both within and outside the Party." (Article 18)

Party leaders are fully aware that their position depends on the acceptance of the people. To maintain Party legitimacy requires continuous communication between Party members and the public. Thus, the CCP constitution has input requirements, such as those in Articles 3 and 18, which require Party members to stay close to the grass roots and inform Party higher-ups about current public opinion. Leadership especially wants to know about growing stresses on the system, such as hostile feelings among the public. Such input is vital for Party management and system persistence.

Democratic Centralism

Both the CCP and the PRC constitutions state that they follow the organizing principle of "democratic centralism." (CCP Article 10, PRC Article 3) In 1906, Lenin quipped, perhaps to a journalist, that "democratic centralism" is "freedom of discussion, unity of action."[13] Of course, there is more to the word "democratic" than "freedom of discussion," just as there is more to the term "centralism" than "unity of action."[14] The Chinese interpret both Marx and Lenin freely, so the CCP constitution elaborates its own meanings for the term "democratic centralism" in several Articles.

China's politics are not like those of the old Soviet Union, and the CCP constitution aspires to have wide participation in decision making precisely so as not to be a top-down Command Organization. In part this aim reflects the ancient custom of "consensus seeking." Reflecting inclusive "democratic" values, higher levels of the Party organization are required to consult with the lower levels that might be effected by a higher level decision. (Article 15) The Party constitution requires, among other things, "meeting-based decision making." (Article 10) Within Party meetings, if there is a significant minority dissenting from the majority view, then for the sake of Party unity and consensus building, "the decision should be delayed and further investigation, research, and exchange of opinions should be undertaken before another vote is held." (Article 17)

What's more, during meetings, members have the right to speak freely, whether critically or constructively, and to "participate in voting and stand for election." (Article 4) But once a decision is made, there should be no public dissent. "Centralism" implies that the central leadership must be obeyed after the "democratic" part has run its course. Also, "Party organizations at all levels shall practice *transparency* in Party affairs." (Article 10) And "Party members in leadership positions at every level, ... do not hold posts for life and can be transferred from or relieved of their posts." (Article 38) These rules, among others, show that for the Chinese, democratic consensus seeking is often more important than having a rigid command structure, as in a military organization.

The Principle of Embedded Leadership

The CCP follows, what I call, the principle of embedded leadership to both stay in touch with the people, and to govern. For instance, one of the duties of CCP members is to form "a Party committee" in any group or organization in society that the Party regards as important for its attention. This can include government agencies or ministries, schools, student organizations, research institutes, provincial and community level organizations, departments of the military, and at all levels of the workplace, from custodial to management, whether private or state owned. (Article 30) These committees, or "Primary-level Party organizations," are *the foundations of Party leadership.* (Article 32, italics added) [15]

As the vanguard of society, their main tasks include keeping the public informed about Party principles and economic and political policies, as well as taking feedback. In-place study groups are encouraged and led by Primary-level Party leaders. Something like union stewards, such leadership includes being available to other Party members in the organization, for consultations, assistance, and supervision, if necessary. These embedded leaders also protect Party members against any infringements of their rights by those above them in the work place.

Another leadership function is to keep an eye out for exceptional talent that can be recruited to help improve Party leadership, especially from among the younger workers. Primary-level Party leaders are also in a position to ensure that Party officials and all other personnel strictly observe state laws and regulations, and not flirt with corruption. (Article 32)

Beyond the tasks like those of union stewards in the West, however, "Party committees will participate on all levels of management decision making and government operations, balancing the needs for the success of the enterprise of which they are a part with the need to implement and comply with Party policies." (Article 33) These rules specifically include having cadres at the very top levels of decision making. (Articles 48-50)

Many, perhaps most, of the officials of the PRC government offices are also members of the Chinese Communist Party (CCP). This includes the NPC, its Standing Committee, the State Council, and the heads of departments, ministries, and agencies. The Communist Youth League has almost as many young members as the full Party membership.[16] Thus, few student organization are without Party members aspiring to leadership.

There are Party branches in most communities. Their leadership must be models of socialist virtue, and they should try to recruit community members who are "revolutionary, *younger*, *better educated*, and *more professional*" than other members of the community. (Articles 34, 35 italics added) There may be over four million grassroots Party organizations spread across the country.[17]

Conclusion: Satisfying the Systemic Requirements

As we have said, at the systemic level, the first problem for evaluative political science is to establish that the specimen under consideration is an actual political system. That is, does it display some minimum amount of political behavior showing evidence of an in-put function, a conversion process, outputs, and feedback in its environment?

In the preceding section I sketched out a profile of China's political system as that is defined by its two constitutions. I mentioned sufficient instances of political behavior to satisfy in a technical way what we all believed intuitively; namely that a political system with Chinese characteristics does exist. The next step in the practice of Normative Political Science is to assess how well the actual operations of the political system satisfy the standards set for it by political science using Easton's definition of the political system as we discussed in Chapter 3.[18]

Part Two: Assessing the Operational Goodness of the Chinese Political System

Extrinsic Goodness

From the extrinsic point of view, the Chinese political system appears differently than it does from the systemic perspective. Systemically, the problem is merely to identify enough political behavior to establish the existence of a political system. In the extrinsic dimension, the focus is more on the details of operations. Following the Logic of Assessment discussed in Chapter 3, an evaluation of a system's extrinsic goodness requires a matching of Easton's definition of a political system, and its constitutive functions, with the political practices on the ground. In this step, political scientists are assessing the operational goodness of the Chinese political system according to standards that are applicable to every political system. Whatever a regime's public relations department may say about the "goodness" of its system, political scientists will make their own assessment, by their own standards.

The task for this research is to determine how well the operation of the political system fulfills each element of the general definition – input, conversion, output, and feedback, all operating within a political, historic, and geographic environment. For example, how well does input information flow into and through the system? How effective is the system at converting inputs into outputs? How successful are outputs at satisfying the prior demands for them? Does feedback flow easily back into the system? The facts about the system's operation will determine the degree of its extrinsic goodness.

Form and Function

For a political science assessment of the extrinsic goodness of a political system's operation, the *form* of the regime is not, in itself, a factor to weigh. In this dimension, the political science focus is on the function, not the form. A researcher, then, looks for how, and how well, the workings of input, conversion, output, and feedback are operating. The words "democracy," "authoritarian," "autocracy," etc. convey no information about either how values are authoritatively allocated, nor how well those operations are functioning. These things can only be known by carefully examining the system at work. So, for assessing the operational goodness of a political system, function, not form, is key. The researcher first looks to see how the elements of a political system are being carried out, and then she or he can assess how well that is being done.

Input

Although the PRC's National People's Congress and the CCP's People's National Congress are not the major sources of law and policy that one would infer from a reading of the two constitutions, they do play a major role in the Chinese political system. They both are broad institutional avenues for input.

As we have seen, filling offices at the basic level for both PRC and CCP begins with popular elections of representatives. These officials then elect those for the next higher group, and so on. Elections are a form of input. The needs, demands, and expectations of the original voters are known to their immediate representatives who convey these up the hierarchy to the very top. Those at the top can also inform themselves about public attitudes through many other sources. These can include visits to provinces, cities, and other local places. Here they can talk to local officials and ordinary folks, as well as make their own observations. The Confucian tradition of consulting widely prior to making policy is also a form of input.[19] As mentioned above, the State Council invites public comments. The press and media are also sources of information for party and government officials to learn about the needs, demands, supports, etc. among the population.

Another institutionalized vehicle for input is the Chinese People's Political Consultative Conference (CPPCC). This is a collection of "civil society" groups all over China which meet for the explicit purpose of enabling people to have a say about whatever political issues concern them. While not made "official" by an Article in either constitution, it has a long history of regular use in the Chinese political system. Public demands, comments, and criticisms can be expressed in these meetings. These communications are then conveyed to leadership in both the PRC and the CCP. Participation is open to all Chinese, rich and poor.[20] Thus, there are many avenues facilitating the flow of input information into the Chinese political system.

Input and Speech

It is likely, and perhaps necessary, that every political system restricts speech, and other forms of individual behavior. As to speech, the types of restrictions depend largely on how regime elites perceive various forms of speech as threats to the persistence of the political system.

In the United States, for example, campaign speech is given broad protection, in part, because having the masses participate in elections and use political speech is regarded as conducive to system persistence. However, since campaigns cost relatively large amounts of money, wealth is generally an advantage for effective input, or participation in public policy discourse, and lack of wealth is a restriction. In Buckley v. Valeo, Citizens United, and other cases, the Supreme Court has found no fault with the clear political advantages in elections that wealth gives to the few who possess it. In Citizens United v. FEC,[21] for example, the High Court held, in effect, that corporations are entitled to the same freedom of speech as individual persons. In the Court's opinion, just as the Constitution's First Amendment prohibits restrictions in political campaigns on the "independent expenditures" of individual persons, so should corporations enjoy the same freedom. Because the masses are tolerant of their disadvantage at making inputs into election campaigns, and the wealthy are pleased with their advantage, the campaign contribution laws create no threats to the persistence of the system and even generate strong support for it.

In China, too, some political speech is restricted. However, the types of restrictions vary from those in the US. In part this is due to the political culture of China. For example, because a high value is placed on achieving consensus prior to making policy decisions, public criticisms of existing policies are perceived as undermining this traditional practice. Disagreement and criticism are encouraged in political meetings because this is a part of the consensus making process. As discussed above, under the heading "Democratic Centralism," several Articles in the CCP Constitution require that freedom of speech be allowed prior to decision making, but restricted thereafter.

There are other historical reasons for China's restrictions on political speech. China has been invaded, and in some places conquered, by foreign nations. Japan took over Manchuria. Great Britain conquered coastal trading cities through both force of arms and by supplying cheap opium to the populations there. They took Hong Cong by force. The United States currently has a hostile stance towards China. Thus, public criticisms of the CCP, the PRC, or of public policies can reasonably be seen as propaganda generated by hostile foreigners meant to undermined the governing regime. Prohibitions of such political speech is meant to avoid the repeating of the past, especially the era which they refer to as the "Century of Humiliation." [22]

The United States also has a history of suppressing speech that the elites regard as threatening to their power. The Supreme Court, in Debs v. United States, upheld the conviction of Eugene V. Debs for doing no more than speaking out against US entry into WWI. For this he was sentenced to 10 years in prison.[23]

While opinions as to the moral propriety of various speech restrictions can be very intense, passing such judgments is not a step in the Normative Political Science method of assessing system goodness. Instead, for the purpose of assessing the operational goodness of the Chinese, or any other, political system, only the facts, not moral judgments, are relevant. Discovering, for example, to what extent, if any, restrictions on speech obstruct the flow of input information in the making of law and policy is important for assessing the operational goodness of a system. Do policy demands flow into the system freely, or are people afraid to express them? Does feedback flow in freely? Also important is learning the degree to which speech restrictions cause resentment and frustration among the members of the system. Determining the extent to which restrictions on input generate stress on the system is an empirical question, which can be addressed by research. Dysfunctional speech restrictions can work to the detriment of a system's operational goodness.

A political system that suppresses, or disregards, the feedback of criticism could be blinding itself to areas in which public hostility is brewing. One possible consequence of such a misguided strategy is that an explosion of public rage might come as a surprise to the leadership. Indeed, this may be what happened in China when students and other reformers seemed to have suddenly filled Tiananmen Square with protests in 1989.[24] The extent to which leadership was surprised by these protests could be an indicator of ineffectiveness, or obstruction, in the input process. An operationally good input process, then, is at least one in which information flows into the system freely enough that the leadership is not caught by surprise with seemingly sudden outbursts of public discontent.

Studies on what sorts of restrictions on input are practiced in the Chinese political system, and the degree to which they lower the operational goodness of the system, have yet to be done. Thus no detailed assessment of how well the input function of the system is operating can be offered at present. However, that the Chinese in general have made an intense and sustained demand for improvement in their conditions and lives cannot be doubted. This was one of the reasons for the broad support of the CCP in the 1949 Revolution. That demand continues, and the support the people continue to give the CCP is largely based on its successful response to it. (This will be discussed further below in the Short History section, and the section on Intrinsic Value.)

Conversion

Easton defines conversion as the process of translating demands on the system into outputs in the form of policies and laws. We have said that the Chinese are strong believers in consultation and consensus building prior to voting on laws and policies. This is the practice for both the PRC and the CCP. The Preamble to the PRC Constitution praises the CPPCC and says that it will continue to play an important role in helping to build China's system of "political consultation." The "General Program," or Preamble, to the CCP constitution declares that, among other things, the

Party shall develop a "consultative democracy."[25] In line with these ideals, the uniquely Chinese input-conversion process is carried out in public discourse and in private communications and numerous meetings held throughout the country.

Ironically, when outsiders view on TV such events as the CCP's National Congress meeting or the National People's Congress of the PRC, it seems that the several hundred attendees all agree in unison with every proposal to be voted on, whether for the election of personnel or for the passage of legislation. Actually, there have been years of prior consultation on each item. This includes many meetings in which tempers may have erupted in ferocious display. But when the decision on an item has been made, local and provincial leaders fall in line. What we see on TV is the climax of consensus building. One of the virtues of this "democratic centralism" for the Chinese is that it satisfies their traditional ideals of consensus building and keeping up the appearance of harmony.

As with TV viewers, it is difficult for political scientists to know, or describe, exactly by what sort of procedure consensus is made prior to voting in the grand meetings. Even though Article 10 of the CCP constitution calls for "transparency," the process seems inscrutable to Western eyes. Without knowing the facts about this procedure, taking the measure of the Chinese political system's conversion process seems to be stumped.[26]

In addition to research on procedure, another way of assessing the goodness of the Chinese conversion process is to examine the public response to its outputs. However inscrutable the procedure, an operationally good conversion process, then, is one which produces outputs that will tend to satisfy critical demands, calm stresses, and build support for the political system. While the Party-State in China seems to have broad avenues over which input information can flow into the system, the regime's sensitivity to, or awareness of, what is most important to the people is tellingly expressed in the outputs that result from the system's conversion process. A dysfunctional process could make the masses feel disregarded and unheard. That could generate hostility among the people, and cause stress for the regime. As we will discuss further below, public satisfaction can, of course, be known through empirical research.

If a governing regime is to sustain its political position, there are, in theory, three ways it can do this. One is by brute force. Another is by brain washing the public with propaganda. A third is by exercising a sufficient degree of skill and wisdom in responding to demand. In practice, a researcher is likely to find some of all three being used in any political system. But the risk of relying heavily on repression is that it will surely stimulate resentment in the members of a system. This could reduce the security of the regime, and increase the chances of revolt or revolution. Propaganda might fool some of the people, but eventually it will be exposed, and stress result.

Clearly, a regime that creates a high degree of stress for itself is likely operating at a diminished capacity, and therefore at a lower degree of goodness than a regime that enjoys the support of its people because it is attentively responsive to their demands. A regime that disregards the desires of the people, or responds to them ineptly, risks allowing hostility to fester. China's "Zero COVID" policy during the pandemic was a cause of significant stress among some of the people. But how much of a threat to system persistence the policy actually caused, and how long lasting the displeasure of the public has been, has yet to be definitively studied.[27] Reflecting CCP values, the policy was meant to save lives, even though the leadership knew it would have harmful effects on the economy. The extent to which the public appreciated these good intentions is also yet to be understood. We will present evidence in the section on intrinsic goodness, below, suggesting that, under the standard of public response, prior to the pandemic, the conversion process in China's Party-State had not been a significant cause of stress, and had been functioning quite well.

Output

Outputs, of course, are the results of the conversion process. This is where the rubber meets the road. Outputs, through their implementation, are tests of how skillfully the regime is responding to the demands and expectations of the public. In theory, that regime which satisfies the most salient demands of the public will have few serious threats from them to its persistence. The Chinese regime seems to be following this principle well enough to have persisted since its official establishment in 1949. Indeed, as I will discuss below, although complicated by its COVID policy, the Party-State appears to be performing its output function very well.

Case studies of how, and how well, specific legislation is implemented, will surely result in varying measures of output goodness. In-depth case studies are not presented here because the aim of this chapter is only to offer an example of how such studies using the Normative Political Science paradigm might be conducted.

Feedback

Feedback can be likened to the test results of an experiment in science. Suppose that output is considered a hypothesis about how to satisfy public demand, and implementation is putting that hypothesis to the test. Then feedback, related to the implementation of an output, is a way by which that hypothesis can be validated or invalidated, in part or in whole. Through cycles of trial and error, a regime can learn what is needed to keep the public sufficiently satisfied so as to stay supportive. A skillful regime will require less hit and miss, or trial and error, attempts than an inept regime.[28]

As we have seen, feedback in China can go into the system through any of the sources of input open to the people. To the extent, if any, that feedback is being disregarded or ineptly managed, stresses on the system can emerge. Identifying such stress and its causes is another matter for empirical research. Case studies can bring to light specific instances of the success or failure of the system to manage feedback. Generally, however, as the section on the intrinsic dimension will show, the Chinese Party-State seems to be generating much more supportive feedback than hostile or negative feedback.

Persistence is Not a Standard of Goodness

As we have said, Easton observes that persistence is a primary aim of a regime in a political system.[29] However, persistence, in itself, is not necessarily an indicator of operational goodness. As mentioned above, a regime can persist through the brutal exercise of state terror. But such persistence would likely generate considerable stress throughout the system. Such stress could result in the build-up of revolutionary resentment that could erupt and bring down the regime. Creating such conditions is surely a dysfunctional way to continue in power.

All political regimes require the use of some degree of force, not just to sustain their political position, but also to maintain social order. Absolute individual liberty is inconsistent with the need for social order. Indeed, one element of every political system is the legitimate use of force. Every political system is unique, so the ways in which force is applied to restrict individual behavior will vary widely. As with restrictions on speech, these will depend on history, custom, current conditions, etc. China, for instance, has its own way of using force to maintain order, just as the US, or Argentina, Britain, etc. have their own ways. Comparing how, and why, force is used in different political systems, and its consequences for a system, can be a subject of great interest and specialty in political science.

The use of force alone need not detract from a system's operational goodness. Government use of force is a type of output, and feedback in response to it can contribute helpful inputs for a regime, provided the regime attends to them properly. A system's public can accept the exercise of force if they regard it as legitimate and appropriate.

Conclusion of the Extrinsic Section

In this section of our assessment of the Chinese political system, we have set out sufficient facts about the political behavior in China to establish, beyond intuition, that there is a political system there. We, of course, used Easton's definition of the political system as our guide in deciding what sort of facts were necessary to show the presence of a political system.

Then we turned again to Easton's definition of the political system, especially as that is expressed in his Flow Chart (Chapter 3), to use as a standard for assessing the performance of each function in the political system. We have found several channels over which inputs flow.[30] We have observed that the conversion process is conducted in a non-Western style, by seeking consensus privately and striving to show harmony publicly. In the absence of details about the operations of this process, public opinion about the outputs enable the political scientist to infer that demands are being at least adequately met by the conversion process. Case studies of the input-output process will have various results depending on the facts of each case. Also, how well the governing regime in China, i.e., the PRC and the CCP, are working together to generate a high degree of synergy in the system is difficult to assess given the regime's penchant for privacy. But the general satisfaction of the members of the political system, i.e., the people, or the public, is a major factor in assessing the over-all goodness of the political system.

Before considering the intrinsic dimension of the system as a whole, it is necessary to look more closely at the historical environment of the Chinese political system. The intrinsic dimension consists of the feelings of the people. To interpret, understand, and explain those feelings requires they be seen in a historical context.

A Short History of the Chinese Political System

The Party-State in China can be said to have begun with the formation of the Communist Party in 1921.[31] Prior to the actual, or official, formation of the Party, many Chinese intellectuals had been participating in study groups, and reading about the Russian Revolution in 1917. Some of them admired what they saw as the success of that Revolution. In Russia, the Communists seemed to have liberated the rural peasantry and urban poor while wresting political power from the Tsar and his wealthy supporters. Among the intellectuals who were inspired by the Russian Revolution was Mao Zedong. Although he was not one of the original founders of the Party, he took part in study groups and learned about Marxism-Leninism, and discussed its application to the circumstances of China.

Also prior to the formation of the Party, great hostility towards the imperial system of rule in China had reached a boiling point. In what came to be known as the "Century of Humiliation," foreign invaders, Great Britain and Japan among them, had forced themselves upon major parts of China. Britain in particular spread opium addiction, and all the invaders exploited workers, merchants, and farmers ruthlessly. Outrage at the weakness and corruption of the imperial system, and the humiliation inflicted by the foreigners, exploded into what came to be known as the Republican Revolution of 1911.

Many future CCP members had fought to overthrow the imperial system, which ended with the abdication of the Empress Dowager. However, the leaders of the Revolution, including Sun Yat-sen and the

Kuomintang party (KMT), failed to establish a national government to replace the imperial system. Fighting between regional and local warlords ensued. In the midst of these conditions, the Communist Party was officially formed by a small group of intellectuals and Republican fighters.

Due to ideological differences, the Kuomintang forces attacked the Communists in 1927. After a few years of intermittent combat, the Red Army was forced to retreat, with the Nationalist Kuomintang in pursuit. The chase wound its way from the central coast, through the heartland, and into the mountains in the north of China, covering roughly 6000 miles. It came to be known as "The Long March."

Mao, and other Communists, took advantage of this trek by teaching the peasantry about the ideals of the new Chinese Communist Party. Mao spoke of how committed the CCP was to the liberation of the downtrodden from the wealthy classes that exploited their labor, and which were supported by the Kuomintang. Mao distinguished himself among CCP membership as a leader, recruiter, and as a propagandist, although he did not officially become Party chairman until 1943.

In the 1930s the Japanese invaded China, raping women, pillaging villages, beating and executing anyone who opposed them. So the Reds stopped fighting with the KMT and in 1937 joined them to fight the Japanese. Soon WWII was on, and that fighting continued until the war's end in 1945.

By this time the Communists had earned the loyalty and gratitude of tens of millions of peasants and workers throughout the land. The Party had made alliances with many other parties, and together they drove the Kuomintang out of mainland China, and on to Taiwan. This was the culmination of the Communist Revolution in 1949. Mao Zedong became a national hero. (To this day, eight of the political parties that had allied themselves to the CCP still function freely in China.)

The formation of the Party-State in China became complete in 1949 when Mao declared the existence of the People's Republic of China (PRC). But there was much to be done. China had gone without an effective national government for a quarter of a century. Wars had raged across the land for most of that time. There was no national economy. Most of the peasantry was extremely poor and had little or no education. There were still remnants of wealthy merchants and landlords exploiting labor.

Strengthening the country by building the economy was the top priority of the new regime. That is what the people demanded, and that is what Mao told the people the CCP would do. Indeed, this *original intention* of the founding fathers of the Chinese Party-State has been a driving force from the start, and remains so today. At first, under Mao's authority, the CCP strove to imitate the example of Stalin in Russia. The government ordered factory constructions, ordered what to produce, and even ordered workers to work in these state owned enterprises. The system had some success at producing needed goods, but agricultural production was dangerously low. So, Mao insisted on a program misnamed "The Great Leap Forward." Rural landlords and merchants were "equalized" with the peasantry by confiscating their wealth and their property. Rural workers were to live in communes. The Party ordered the planting of the crops it deemed needed.

As a result of this program, crops failed to grow as expected, harvests were poor, and a terrible famine followed. By the mid-1960s as many as 50 million people had starved to death. Dissent began to increase among both the public and the Party leadership. Mao felt threatened. In response, he reached out to the populace, which still regarded him as a Liberating Hero, and called for assistance to quell what he saw as the counter-revolutionary capitalist backlash. Young Communists all over the country began attacking anyone known to have criticized Mao. There were beatings, murders, and public humiliations. Universities and schools were shut down. Professors and Party elites were sent to work among the peasants and to live in rural communes. This "Cultural Revolution" lasted until Mao's death in 1976.

Of course, most of those Party leaders who were sent to the farm were not "capitalists." Many of them had trekked alongside Mao in the Long March, and had fought in the 1949 Revolution. They were committed Communists. But they could see that Mao's Stalinist approaches to economic reform were the wrong way to go. After Mao's death, these former Party leaders re-grouped. They had the leaders of the Cultural Revolution arrested and prosecuted, including the infamous "Gang of Four." One of them was Mao's fourth wife, Jiang Qing, who was arrested in 1976, and imprisoned. She committed suicide in 1991.[32]

Among the re-grouped CCP leaders was Deng Xiaoping. He had been an early advocate of experimenting with economic free trade zones, and with letting farmers sell some of their crops for a profit. Now he wanted the entire country to experiment with these economic policies. But there were still old-line Maoists in Party and PRC leadership positions who opposed deviating from the Stalinist approach. To go around their obstinacy, Deng devised a clever plan. In 1992, he mentioned to some friends and colleagues that he needed a rest, and that he was taking his family on a vacation to enjoy the Southern coastal areas of China.

Under that cover he travelled around these areas confronting every old comrade he knew from their shared revolutionary past. Individually he challenged them to "stop acting like old women with bound feet."[33] He argued that the Party had sufficient control of the country so that it could safely relax the restraints on businesses and capital financing by foreigners, and also unleash the entrepreneurship of the Chinese people.

Deng's "Southern Tour" was a smashing success. Reformers overcame opposition, repealed constricting laws, and enacted pro-growth legislation. Every province and city followed suit. Investment funds came pouring in. Factories that had been ordered by Mao to make military parts, quickly turned to auto parts, and parts for trucks and buses. Railroad lines were laid across the country. Due, in large part, to the new trading and traveling, a national economy spread like wildfire. New apartment buildings shot up to accommodate the millions of rural folks coming to cities to work. Workers had money to spend. Soon even the old grey "Mao jackets" were trashed in favor of the newest European styles.

Life after Deng Xiaoping

In 2022, the World Bank released a report entitled "Four Decades of Poverty Reduction in China." The study found that "extreme poverty has been eliminated" in China. It states that since the early 1980s, the income for "close to 800 million" people has risen above "the International Poverty Line as defined by the World Bank."[34] Thus, starting from a base line at which the masses were living in extreme poverty, with millions starving to death, China has grown a massive middle class. The World Bank notes that China's leadership intends to keep up this improvement momentum, and to strive to eliminate all poverty while further raising the standard of living for its vast middle class.

Life expectancy in China has more than doubled since the CCP won the Revolution in 1949. Before then it was a mere 35 years. But by 2015, it had increased nationally to 76.3 years. Among all the provinces, Shanghai ranks first, reaching to 82.8 in 2015.[35] And, China's official TV station recently announced that, "As of 2020, basic medical insurance covers more than 1.3 billion people …"[36]

The Cultural Revolution had closed numerous schools and universities, in some cases for 10 years, prior to Mao's death in 1976. Illiteracy was widespread. But in the summer of 2022, China's Ministry of Education announced that 240 million people have since received at least some higher education, and that the current "number of students in higher education at present is more than 44.3 million."[37] China now has more highly educated people than any other country on Earth, including the USA.

Thus, while political scientists may regret that the Party-State's exact law and policy making procedures remain opaque, the regime's conversion process has produced policy outputs that are not only responsive to the expectations of the people for economic improvement, but their success far exceeds what anyone demanded or thought was possible, and even exceed what was promised. Those government policies have been an important contributing cause of China's "economic miracle" in large part because they unleashed the energy, determination, and entrepreneurial genius of the Chinese people.

Policy Output as Primary Cause of Growth

Since Deng Xiaoping, China's "market socialism," as managed by the Party-State, has wisely combined the "odd bedfellows" of government intervention in the economy – to alleviate poverty, to stimulate investment, and to protect some state owned enterprises – with selectively allowing less regulated markets to drive growth. While rejecting some of Mao's command economy policies, Deng had presciently argued that a socialist regime could allow elements of a market economy without having to endure the exploitations of capitalism.[38]

As Harvard professor of Political Economy, Dani Rodrik, has observed, China's "Economic Miracle" is not a miracle at all. It is the result of a very smart Industrial Policy. Indeed, "a mixed, state-driven economic model has always been at the root of Chinese economic success." Contrary to both the old British Adam Smith Liberalism, and the current US Neoliberalism, such as that of John Williamson's "Washington Consensus," Rodrik shows, with examples, how the brilliant industrial policy of China's leadership explains the Economic Miracle of China's great growth.[39] The World Bank, too, gives credit to China's Party-State governing when it states that the "success of China's economic development and the associated reduction of poverty benefited from effective governance, which helped coordinate multiple government agencies and induce cooperation from non-government stakeholders."[40] Perhaps that report can stand as evidence of synergy, and the absence of harmful friction, in the operation of the Chinese political system.

The Authoritative Allocation of Values

The task of every political system, as Easton notes, is the authoritative allocation of values. But, as China has shown, this does not necessarily mean that the government does all the allocating of values through its own agencies. A government can allow the allocation of values through other means, such as through markets, while at the same time keeping economic activity on the path of benefiting the people. Pursuant to this strategy the CCP has recently pledged to "remain committed to *a people-centered philosophy of development*."[41] This philosophy goes beyond crass materialism, and, echoing the humanism of the young Karl Marx, aims to take economic development in the direction of making "more notable and substantive progress toward achieving *well-rounded human development* and common prosperity for all."[42]

Continuity of CCP Policy

Of course, as China develops, new problems will emerge to challenge leadership. The COVID pandemic is a recent example of that. So as each new CCP leader takes his position (and there have been no women in the very top jobs), he faces conditions and priorities somewhat different than did his predecessor. For example, in the early stages of rapid growth, corruption might have been tolerated while more growth-producing matters were attended to, such as encouraging banks to be more generous with their loan practices, and inviting foreign investment. But as those early growth policies succeeded, more attention could be turned to anti-corruption measures. This was the case for Xi Jinping, who became Secretary General of the CCP in 2012, and PRC president in 2013. Since then, he has led a major crackdown on corruption. Indeed, in just his first three years in office, more than 100,000 people, including many top officials, have been arrested, charged, convicted, and punished for corruption.[43]

As new CCP leaders come into office, the custom has been for them to give new names to their particular programs, but also to show the continuity of principle and promise between their agenda and the original intentions of the CCP founders. For example, Xi Jinping introduced the term "Chinese Dream," to suggest he has some new policies to take on some of the new challenges facing the country's continuing development. But he has also stated, "Our Party's history is a history of continuously adapting Marxism to the Chinese context." He added that throughout its 100 year history, the CCP "has been of one mind with the people."[44]

In other words, the original policy of Mao and the founding fathers of the Chinese Party-State has remained the commitment to follow Marxist-Leninism in making life more livable for the people by improving conditions and strengthening the nation through economic reform. Even while criticizing Mao's strategy for attaining those ends, Deng Xiaoping, as we have seen, shared Mao's original intent. This is why a recent release of official Party history begins with these words, "Since its founding in 1921, the Communist Party of China (CPC) has remained true to its original aspiration and mission of seeking happiness for the Chinese people and rejuvenation for the Chinese nation."[45]

Nevertheless, the different labels used for the agendas of in-coming Party leaders have confused some anti-CCP commentators, who then claim the Party is chameleon-like, simply saying whatever they think will maintain Party legitimacy among a naïve and gullible people.[46] But this is clearly untrue. The Party-State has not wavered from the original intentions of its founders. Even its 2022 COVID-19 policy of shutting down large areas to stop the spread of the disease, shows the "people centered philosophy" that the health of humans is more important to the regime than pursuing the growth of GDP.[47]

Beyond the Numbers

Analyses of China's "economic miracle," when done from the economics point of view, appear to be insensitive to the *human dimension* of the regime's achievement; that is, the realization of the aim to use government power to improve human welfare by developing the economy. What does it mean in human terms that roughly 800 million individual human beings were guided in lifting themselves out of the grinding poverty, and even famine, which is from where they started their ascent?

Agony

One answer to this question is that along with the growth of GNP came a liberation from the kind of suffering that plagued the Chinese in their prior conditions. In other words, hundreds of millions of individuals were freed from numerous causes of agony. These painful feelings include the grief of needless infant mortality, the aches for the want of food and unfilled material desire, and the feelings of helplessness and frustration of being entrapped in poverty for life.[48]

Joy

Regime economic policy, including CCP embedded leadership, has empowered a population of more than twice that of the United States to enjoy, in addition to their new economic security, more births of healthy babies, greater health and extended longevity for all, and education levels never before seen in China's long history. Options for individual self-realization have multiplied many fold in their new complex economy. Life for the Chinese people has been made more secure and enjoyable by CCP policies. This is the *humanitarian* dimension of China's "economic miracle," which numbers alone cannot convey.

Putting the "Miracle" into Perspective

As we have seen, the regime's humanitarian intentions have been fulfilled to such an extent that China's success may be without equal in the history of the human race. Through the operations of the political system, nearly 800 million people have been empowered to build for themselves the largest middle class in the world. How can the enormity of this humanitarian achievement be put into perspective? Is there any other humanitarian act in history that compares to this?

One example of a well-known great humanitarian achievement was primarily carried out by the United States just after the conclusion of WWII. Then, in perhaps its finest hour, the United States of America sought to lend a helping hand to the devastated people of Europe; but the US government also magnanimously reached out to help its former foes, Germany, Italy, and Japan.

This was done primarily through the Marshal Plan, the Berlin Airlift, and related legislation enacted and implemented late in the Democratic administration of Harry Truman, and continued in the early Republican administration of Dwight D. Eisenhauer.

The Berlin Airlift, 1948–1949

After the defeat of Hitler's Germany, the Allies and the Soviet Union disagreed about which side would take control of Berlin. In a moment of pique, the Soviets threw up a blockade that prevented Allied access by rail, road, and water to the city. Over two million Germans were forced to try and live in the ruins, including through winter, without sufficient food, shelter, clothing, or the materials they needed to recover from war devastation.

Even though the Germans had been their wartime enemies, the US, working with some allies, defied the blockade by airlifting food and other supplies to Berlin from Allied airbases in western Germany. In 1949, after nearly a year of parachuting in supplies, the Soviets relented, allowing supplies into Eastern Berlin, which they had walled off.[49]

The Marshall Plan, 1945–1952

Pursuant to the Marshall Plan, and related assistance programs, the US Congress appropriated over $13 billion in economic recovery funds to help Western European economies, including Germany and Italy.[50] That is the equivalent in purchasing power of about $160 billion in 2022 money.[51] The funds went to food, clothing, capital investments, materials for rebuilding, and the costs of sending US business advisors. While economists may debate the precise impact of the Marshall Plan on Western European economies, the good will it generated is incalculable, and so is the transfer of American business know-how.

Historians all over the world have recognized it as a great humanitarian achievement. Indeed, Secretary of State Marshall became the only former military general ever to receive a Nobel Peace Prize.[52] Additional legislation was enacted to help Japan.

During the period in which US reconstruction programs were being implemented, Europe had a population of around 550 million, and Japan about 83 million.[53] Thus, US post-war assistance helped roughly 633 million people to build the strong economies they now enjoy. Of course, not all 633 million Europeans and Japanese lifted themselves to a middle class level. Nevertheless, the people of these countries today are beneficiaries of the great humanitarian programs of the USA in mid-twentieth century.

Calling Winners in the Competition of Good

Comparing the humanitarian achievements of the US post-WWII and those of China currently can invite the question as to which is the greater achievement. For the US, one can argue that it may have benefited fewer people, but it acted with unsurpassed magnanimity in victory, by providing generous assistance to its former enemies, Germany, Italy, and Japan. For China, one can argue that, just going by the numbers, the Party-State's vast and rapidly attained humanitarian achievements easily rank with, if not out rank, those of the Marshall Plan Era. Whatever sides are taken, historians will likely agree, however, that the humanitarian achievements of both nations are without peers in history. (Perhaps the invention of vaccinations is a greater humanitarian achievement because of the numbers of humans helped. But we are only comparing the achievements of nations here.)

Assessing Goodness

Although it is not flawless, if the operational goodness of the Chinese political system is judged by its success at converting public demands for increased economic well-being into responsive policy, with actual results in the lives of many millions of human beings, then we may reasonably say that the system has achieved a substantial degree of operational, or extrinsic, goodness. In this sense, the system can be assessed as performing very well.

An additional standard by which to assess the goodness of the Chinese political system is to use the surveys of public opinion that ask how members feel about life within their system. This will be the aim of the next section. Here, again, the measure of goodness will be based on the facts about public opinion, as those are found by social scientists.

Part Three: The Intrinsic Dimension of the Chinese Political System

Political Happiness in China

Xi Jinping has said that "only the wearer of the shoes knows if they fit or not. The Chinese people know best whether the Chinese socialist system suits the country or not."[54] While that may be true, how is a political scientist researcher to know if the self-reports of Chinese political happiness are authentic, or are instead given from fear, or the result of propaganda and "brain washing"?[55]

How authentically satisfied people are with life in their political system is an empirical question. Large surveys can be helpful for gathering an overview. But to evaluate the authenticity of self-reports about political satisfaction requires the mixed methods of interpretive political science. These methods bring the political scientist closer to the subjects where nonverbal clues to authenticity, or its opposite, fear based dissembling, can be detected. Of the many pre-COVID studies of Chinese attitudes and opinion, for example, just a few recent ones will be cited as indicators of Chinese political sentiments.

The Zang Study

The first study to be considered is by Leizhen Zang, of the School of Public Policy and Management, at the University of Chinese Academy of Sciences, Beijing, China, published in 2020.

Zang's study found that, among other things, "China's middle class's trust in governments has increased. For example, in China, trust in the national government reaches 97% and trust in local governments is at

79%." Over 82% of "the Chinese middle class are proud of their state." When asked if they "would rather live under their system of government than any other," approximately 77% affirmed that they are "willing to live under their system of government, [and] more than half of the respondents state that their system of government does not need to be changed." While "Internet use is regulated by the government to a certain extent in China … 49% of the Chinese middle class … still have accesses to more information, especially negative news about the Chinese government." Despite their exposure to criticisms of the Party-State, studies show that "they do not have the willingness to promote political changes."[56]

The Harvard Study

A 2016 Harvard study of Chinese public opinion found that, "95.5 percent of respondents were either 'relatively satisfied' or 'highly satisfied' with Beijing."[57] The authors consider the responses to have been authentic, and express their doubt that they were based on fear or propaganda. They explain that "Although state censorship and propaganda are widespread in China, these findings highlight that citizen perceptions of governmental performance respond most to real, measurable changes in individuals' material well-being." In addition, "China is still a developing country … We tend to forget that for many in China, and in their lived experience of the past four decades, each day was better than the next." In effect, the authors are saying that the poll results show a people who are well satisfied with the outputs made in response to their prior demands for economic improvement.

However, material conditions alone do not account for political satisfaction in China. "The surveys found that rural residents, generally poorer than those in cities, had more optimistic attitudes about inequality than their wealthier urban counterparts." The authors conclude, "Our surveys show that many in China therefore seem to be much more satisfied with government performance over time, despite rising inequality, corruption, and a range of other pressures that are the result of the reform era." The authors comment that in contrast to Chinese public opinion, a recent Gallup poll in the US found that "only 38 percent of respondents were satisfied with the federal government."

Pew Research

Independent of the Harvard study, a 2016 Pew Research survey found that, on balance, "the Chinese public is optimistic" about the likely improvement of their political conditions.[58] "A 64% majority believes corruption will lessen over the next five years; only 19% think it will get worse." However, some softness in the optimism shows up in the finding that "40% think the gap between rich and poor will get better, while 37% expect it to grow worse."

Nonetheless, the "public is also optimistic about the long-term economic future. Roughly eight-in-ten (82%) [of the Chinese] think that when children in the country today grow up they will be financially better off than their parents." On that measure, the Pew researchers comment that the Chinese "positive outlook stands in stark contrast to the pessimism found in the United States and much of Europe." Indeed, far from wanting political change, "roughly three-quarters (77%) of Chinese believe that their way of life needs to be protected against foreign influence." Indeed, the survey shows that the Chinese respondents are especially worried about the designs of the United States. "Fully 45% of Chinese see U.S. power and influence as posing a major threat to their country. Such concern is up from 39% in 2013."

Conclusion

One lesson to be learned from this chapter is that a political system cannot be fully understood without including the facts of public affect. As Easton emphasized, a political system is about human life. Therefore, the study of how well a political system is working is incomplete without an account of how the folks living in it feel about life within it. Ideally, then, a system would be working at its best when all its members feel that the system is sustaining and enhancing their lives. Hence, where political unhappiness is found, the research problem becomes tracing its causes in the operation of the political system. Perhaps, then, the main contribution of the Easton-Hartman Synthesis is to make the consideration of public sentience a regular step in the application of the interpretive framework for Normative Political Science.

This approach grounds the assessment of a political system's goodness in the empirical examination of facts. The factual study of a people's political feelings requires the use of the mixed methods of interpretive political science, as opposed to either large impersonal surveys, or assessing "goodness" with lofty, but vaguely defined, philosophical ideals like "democracy," "socialism," "liberty," "justice," etc. In other words, how the people living in a political system authentically feel about their experience in it is a more sensitive measure of a system's goodness than determining how well a system's formal institutions conform to some preferred philosophical ideal.[59]

Finally, in the section on the systemic dimension we noted that the two constitutions of the Chinese Party-State appear to put few limitations on the ability of the Party elite to act as they wish. While they have so far proven to both solicit and consider public input, and have generally acted unselfishly and in the best interests of the Chinese people, the constitutional safeguards against future governmental abuses seem flimsy. It seems risky for a political system, like China's, to depend on the hope that future generations of leaders will be as public regarding as were the Founders of the Party-State, and as are their current successors.

While often imperfect, political institutions, well crafted, may provide better assurance of future leadership for the people as a whole, than lofty hopes based on weak constitutions, like those of China's. Our analysis of China's systemic dimension suggests some need for institutional improvements. But this critique rests upon the unproven assumption that institutions can guarantee civic minded leadership in future times. However, it appears that if future Chinese Party-State leadership continues to make the wise decisions that have done so much for the people, and have thereby kept the regime, particularly the CCP, in the high regard of the system's membership, then it seems likely that the regime could persist in position for a period as long as the Catholic Church was a reigning power in Europe, which it was for roughly 1000 years. [60]

Endnotes

[1] Easton, 1953, 1967a, 1967b.
[2] Hartman, 1967; and Kelleher 2020.
[3] Easton, 1967a, 1967b.
[4] Constitution of the People's Republic of China. (Full text after amendment on March 14, 2004) People's National Congress Website.
http://www.npc.gov.cn/zgrdw/englishnpc/Constitution/node_2825.htm
[5] News and information about the structure and operations of the People's National Congress can be found on the official NPC website at, http://www.npc.gov.cn. For the History of The National People's Congress of the People's Republic of China, http://www.npc.gov.cn./npc/c234/list.shtml
The NPC Observer is an informative blog covering the National People's Congress (NPC) and its Standing Committee (NPCSC). Changhao Wei founded NPC Observer in October 2016. See note 30, below.
https://npcobserver.com
[6] See Truex 2016; Gandhi et al 2020; and Lu et al 2020.
[7] State Council. Official website. https://english.www.gov.cn/statecouncil/
[8] In 2021, offices and departments under the State Council handled 8,666 suggestions from NPC deputies and 5,718 proposals submitted by CPPCC members. A report to Li Keqiang stated that State Council departments adopted more than 4,300 pieces of advice and subsequently introduced over 1,600 policy measures.
"Premier urges gathering of wisdom to improve govt work." Xinhua News Agency. Feb 15,2022.

http://english.www.gov.cn/premier/news/202202/15/content_WS620baab9c6
d09c94e48a5138.html

9. See Zhong Yan 2018.

10. The 20th National Congress of the Communist Party of China adopted the revised Constitution of the CCP on Oct 22, 2022. Updated: October 26, 2022. The full text of the CCP Constitution can be found on the State Council website at,
http://english.www.gov.cn/news/topnews/202210/26/content_WS635921cdc
6d0a757729e1cd4.html

While the term "constitution" is used for both the PRC and the CCP documents, the second usage is somewhat anomalous. At least since Aristotle, the word "constitution" has been used, in a political context, to refer to the organization of a political system's regime. In American English, the CCP document might more aptly be called the Party "by-laws," or "Articles of Incorporation" because it does not establish formal government institutions, but only its own rules. I follow the English convention which is to use the abbreviation "CCP" rather than "CPC" for the Chinese Communist Party.

Notice of elections for the Party's 20th National Congress November 19, 2021. People's Daily Online,
http://politics.people.com.cn/n1/2021/1119/c1001-32286217.html

12. This order of authority is my effort to clarify relationships that are not entirely clear in Article 23. The CCP constitution uses the term "Political Bureau," rather than "politburo," presumably as a part of its efforts to distance itself from Soviet practice.

13. Lenin, Vladimir (1906). "Report on the Unity Congress of the R.S.D.L.P." "VIII. The Congress Summed Up". Marxists Internet Archive.
https://www.marxists.org/archive/lenin/works/1906/rucong/viii.htm

Lenin was not the first writer to use this term, and his first known usage was not in the original 1902 edition of *What is to be Done?* See, "Lenin and Democratic Centralism." April 12, 2013. SocialistWorker.org
https://socialistworker.org/blog/critical-reading/2013/04/12/meaning-
democratic-centralism

14. See note 39 below re the various meanings of the terms "democratic" and "democracy."

15. Pieke, Frank N. 2009. *The Good Communist Elite Training and State Building in Today's China*. Cambridge: Cambridge University Press. pp. 29–30: "The recruitment and deployment of cadres is one of the most important ways in which the party-state integrates itself with society and guides and directs the project of socialist transformation."

______. 2016. Knowing China: A Twenty-First Century Guide. Cambridge University Press.

[16] Heilmann (2017), 63.

[17] Ibid., 62. The China scholar, Sebastian Heilmann, suggests that "the PRC was conceived of as an executive instrument of the party." He also suggests that the establishment of two constitutions, with the CCP being the leading body, facilitates "an explicit rejection of political limitations on power." Heilmann 2017, pages 56 and 57.

[18] While Normative Political Science sets the standard for assessing the operational goodness of any political system, that is not the only standard by which to take assessments. For instance, every nation sets a standard for itself as a part of its regime. This can be considered its constitution. Some nations, like the USA, have a written constitution. Assessments can be made as to how well the political behavior on the ground fulfills this standard. As we have seen, China has two written constitutions. Other nations, such as Britain and Israel, have no written constitution. Unlike assessing the operational goodness of a political system, constitutional goodness can be assessed in a strictly formal way without considering the feelings of the people.

[19] On the philosophical effort to reconcile traditional Confucianism with Marxism see, Yang, Y. (2023). Confucianism and Common Prosperity (2023). In: China and the West. Palgrave Macmillan, Singapore. https://doi.org/10.1007/978-981-99-1882-9_12

[20] Schum 2021. And see note 6, above. The CPPCC is praised in the PRC Preamble. See note 4 for link.

[21] *Buckley v. Valeo*, 424 U.S. 1 (1976), Citizens United v. FEC, 558 U.S. 310 (2010).

[22] See the article in Wikipedia about China's Century of Humiliation at, https://en.wikipedia.org/wiki/Century_of_humiliation

[23] *Debs v. United States*, 249 U.S. 211

[24] See the article in Wikipedia about Tiananmen Square at, https://en.wikipedia.org/wiki/Tiananmen_Square

[25] See notes 4 and 10, above

[26] See Truex, note 6, regarding some examples of what is known about China's policy making process.

[27] There is a sea of information on the subject. A Google search on the policy shows over one million links to news and journalistic commentary. A Google Scholar search shows nearly a half million links.

[28] Truex 2016 is a case study of how food safety laws were developed, and it gives examples of feedback operating in the legislative process of China's political system.

29. I use the word "aim" not as a goal or end point but as a guide to problem recognition, problem solving, and decision making for the operative parties of the regime.

30. One excellent source of insight into the flow of information in the PRC legislative process is the NPC Observer. See, for example, "Term Review: How Long Did It Take the 13th NPC to Pass a Law?" May 1, 2023. Changhao Wei & Taige Hu
https://npcobserver.com/2023/05/01/china-npc-bill-law-legislative-time/ See note 5, above.

31. This summary history is based on a variety of sources. See note 3 above. The Preamble for both the PRC and the CCP constitutions. And, the official history of the period adopted at the Sixth Plenary Session of the 19th Central Committee of the Communist Party of China on November 11, 2021. See, "Resolution of the CPC Central Committee on the Major Achievements and Historical Experience of the Party over the Past Century." Xinhua News Agency. October 16, 2021.
http://www.news.cn/english/2021-11/16/c_1310314611.htm

32. "Suicide of Jiang Qing, Mao's Widow, Is Reported." Nicholas D. Kristof. NYT. June 5, 1991.
https://www.nytimes.com/1991/06/05/obituaries/suicide-of-jiang-qing-mao-s-widow-is-reported.html

33. "Deng Xiaoping's famous speeches." Globaltimes.cn Published: 2012-2-16
https://www.globaltimes.cn/content/696154.shtml#:~:text=We%20must%20not%20act%20like,and%20create%20a%20new%20path.

34. "Over the past 40 years, the number of people in China with incomes below … the International Poverty Line as defined by the World Bank … has fallen by close to 800 million. … In 2021, China declared that it has eradicated extreme poverty according to the national poverty threshold …" p. viii.
"Four Decades of Poverty Reduction in China." World Bank Group. Development Research Center of the State Council, The People's Republic of China. Conference Edition. 2022
https://thedocs.worldbank.org/en/doc/bdadc16a4f5c1c88a839c0f905cde802-0070012022/original/Poverty-Synthesis-Report-final.pdf
Also, "more than 800 million people have been lifted out of poverty" p.i. "The World Bank in China." The World Bank Report. April 2022.
https://www.worldbank.org/en/country/china/overview

35. Chen, H., Hao, L., Yang, C. et al. "Understanding the rapid increase in life expectancy in shanghai, China: a population-based retrospective analysis." *BMC Public Health* 18, 256 (2018). https://doi.org/10.1186/s12889-018-5112-7

36. CGTN re: website basic medical insurance,

https://www.cgtn.com/how-china-works/feature/What-does-staying-true-to-the-founding-mission-mean-for-the-CPC.html

37. "China establishes world's largest higher education system with 240 million college graduates." Global Times. May 17, 2022. https://www.globaltimes.cn/page/202205/1265868.shtml

38. See note 17, above.

39. Rodrik "China as Economic Bogeyman." Dani Rodrik. Project Syndicate. Jul 9, 2020. https://prosyn.org/hP5ue5P In a landmark study, Rodrik shows how government industrial policy and legislation, when wisely applied, stimulated growth in Asian countries, but had little effect when ineptly applied elsewhere. "The 'Paradoxes' of the Successful State." Dani Rodrik. *European Economic Review* 41 (1997) 411-442.
https://www.sciencedirect.com/science/article/pii/S0014292197000123

40. China became a member of the World Bank in 1980. It started "as a recipient of support from the International Development Association (IDA), the Bank Group's fund for the poorest [countries]." By 1999 China no longer drew upon World Bank support, and it "became a donor in 2007." It is now the World Bank's third largest shareholder. "The World Bank In China." See note 19, above.

41. See CCP Official History, note 15 italics added. Also, to the extent that the word "democracy" is used in the translations of Chinese political speech it can have different connotations than that in the West, which primarily means frequent elections of officials. A personal communication from a native Chinese speaker, Jun 14, 2022, explains, "In Chinese '民主' isn't really translate into 'democracy.' '民主,' pronounced minzhu, means 'people first.' If you put 'minzhu' in government, people generally have misconception of 'democracy government,' actually the proper meaning is people-centric government, the government that serves people. Democracy government in our term simply means '选举制政府,' so called popular voted government, [that] doesn't really mean people-centric wholeheartedly. That's why China's full country name is People's Republic of China. A republic country that serve it's people." For an expanded discussion of the meaning of the word "democracy" in Chinese see, Perry 2015.

42. Re the humanism of the young Marx see, Fromm (1961), and Smith (1996)

43. "Robber barons, beware". The Economist. October 24, 2015. Archived without paywall in The Wayback Machine,
https://web.archive.org/web/20171213182557/https://www.economist.com/news/china/21676814-crackdown-corruption-has-spread-anxiety-among-chinas-business-elite-robber-barons-beware

44. Xi Focus: Xi stresses studying Party history as CPC gears up for centenary. Xinhua News Agency. 2021-02-20
http://www.xinhuanet.com/english/2021-02/20/c_139755103.htm

[45] See CCP Official History, note 15

[46] One example of the pro-Western view that the CCP's rhetoric is mere pragmatism, without ideology, see: Brown (2012)

[47] Reuters reports that economists anticipated a slowing of growth in China due to zero tolerance COVID policy. "China to use effective investment, not flood-like stimulus, to boost economy, state media report."
Reuters. July 29, 2022
https://www.reuters.com/business/autos-transportation/china-extends-tax-exemption-electric-cars-state-media-says-2022-07-29/

[48] I use an empathic interpretation of how the Chinese likely felt because empirical studies of these feelings are not readily available.

[49] The Berlin Airlift, 1948–1949. US State Department. History Section.
https://history.state.gov/milestones/1945-1952/berlin-airlift

[50] The US National Archives, "Marshall Plan (1948)," at, p13
https://www.archives.gov/milestone-documents/marshall-plan?_ga=2.119524425.1720170315.1659567268-125933810.1659567268

[51] This amount is according to the Inflation Calculator, p13
https://www.in2013dollars.com/ ,
https://www.in2013dollars.com/us/inflation/1950?amount=13

[52] The Marshall Plan, 1945–1952 at, p14
https://history.state.gov/milestones/1945-1952/marshall-plan

[53] According to Our World in Data, the population of Europe was 549.82 million in 1950.
https://ourworldindata.org/grapher/world-population-by-world-regions-post-1820.
According to Historical World Population Data, compiled by Wm. Robert Johnston, Europe's population was 549.043 million in 1950.
http://www.johnstonsarchive.net/other/worldpop.html
According to an official site for Japanese Government Statistics, the population of Japan in 1950 was about 83.2 million, https://www.e-stat.go.jp/en/stat-search?page=1&query=population%201950 at
file:///C:/Users/18188/Downloads/50a00100.pdf

[54] Quote provided in a personal communication to the author. Its source can be found at, Xi Focus-Quotable Quotes: Xi Jinping on modernization of China's system, capacity for governance. Xinhua News Agency. Oct. 10, 2020.
http://english.ts.cn/system/2020/10/10/036459085.shtml

[55] For a skeptical view, see Wallace (2016).

[56] Zang, L. 2020. "Middle Class and Its Attitude Toward Government in Different Political Systems: A Comparison of China and Japan." *Chinese Political Science Review*, 5(1), 74–94. https://doi.org/10.1007/s41111-018-0115-1 One problem

with the use of the term "middle class" is that Chinese authorities are reluctant to agree to the term. In part, because it implies class divisions and status divisions which conflict with the ideals of the Party-State. An additional problem for Zang's study is that his criteria for education, income, and occupation used to classify respondents as "middle class" would actually put them in the range of upper middle class in an American understanding. His use of "a standard questionnaire," may suggest the above average literacy of the respondents who completed it. Follow up "interviews were conducted in local languages." Most of the data was collected before 2012. Quotes from Zang are taken from Section 3.1 Data Description, and Section 3.2 Empirical Results. Page numbers are not available online.

[57.] "Taking China's Pulse: Ash Center research team unveils findings from long-term public opinion survey." Dan Harsha. *Ash Center Communications*. July 9, 2020. https://news.harvard.edu/gazette/story/2020/07/long-term-survey-reveals-chinese-government-satisfaction/ All quotes from same study. Page numbers for quotes not available online.

[58.] "Chinese Public Sees More Powerful Role in World, Names U.S. as Top Threat." *Pew Research Center Report*. October 5, 2016. Richard Wike and Bruce Stokes. https://www.pewresearch.org/global/2016/10/05/chinese-public-sees-more-powerful-role-in-world-names-u-s-as-top-threat/ All quotes from same study. Page numbers for quotes not available online. The use of the three studies mentioned in the text is an elementary form of "triangulation," which is a way of validating empirical claims made in Interpretive social science. See Carter et al. 2014.

[59.] American political science is currently haunted by a Puritan Spirit, especially in its studies of China. Although feigning to be "neutral" observers, throughout the literature scholars use "democracy" as a term of moral praise, and "authoritarianism" as a term of moral condemnation. For examples see note 6 and note 35 above. But in Normative Political Science, as we have said, such moral terms are eschewed in favor of focusing on how well a system operates, and on how authentically satisfied the members are with their experience of living within a system. Also see the discussion of form and function in the text.

[60.] Mark, Joshua J. "The Medieval Church." World History Encyclopedia. Last modified June 17, 2019. https://www.worldhistory.org/Medieval_Church/ Having helped raise some 800M people out of poverty and into a thriving middle class, the Chinese Party-State is probably the most beneficent government any country has ever had.

Chapter Five:

Normative Political Science and the Organization of the Profession

Introduction

We have seen in the preceding chapters what the Normative Political Science paradigm consists of, and how to apply it as a research framework. The Easton-Hartman Synthesis combines Robert S. Hartman's conception of value science with David Easton's theory of the political system. While Easton only envisioned his theory of the political system as a guide to empirical research in political science, using his axiom as a rule of relevancy, the model of Hartman's value science enables us to propose an additional application of Easton's definition of the political system. We have shown that this definition can also be used as *a standard* for assessing the operational goodness of a political system. Of course, the facts about how a system operates must be known before an assessment of how well it operates can be made. In this approach, facts are the measure of value.

Characteristically, as a global thinker, Easton's vision for political science reached beyond just defining the concept of the political system. His vision encompassed an organizational plan for the political science profession with the study of the political system as but one of its defining objectives. We will discuss that plan in this chapter.

Easton understood that making an organizational plan for the political science profession can begin by addressing such questions as "what is the purpose of political science?" or "what is political science useful for?" More than just to study the political system, Easton saw political science as a way of serving a moral motivation. He learned from his experience in, and studies of, the field that from its beginning the "inspiration behind political science is clearly ethical."[1] But the ethical, or moral, motivation can be a two edge sword.

As we saw in Chapter 1, Easton rejected equilibrium theory as a central concept for political science. One of his criticisms is that, in practice, it often acted as "a concealed ethical premise."[2] This covert ethical, or moral, position could have distorting effects on the way political behavior was perceived. In such cases, morally "good" political behavior was that which facilitates equilibrium. Looking for this, the attention of the political scientist could easily be drawn to what appears as anomalous behavior deserving criticism. Studies of American politics, for example, could depict negotiating behavior among insider elites as if normal, and good for preserving equilibrium. But "intransigent," or noncooperative, behavior by outsider groups could be seen as aberrant, threatening to upset the equilibrium. Here, the a priori moral assumption that political behavior *ought to* tend towards equilibrium prejudices the mind of the researcher. Instead of trying to weigh the justifications a group might have for disrupting the equilibrium, the "empirical" problem becomes explaining why that behavior has gone "wrong."[3] Thus, equilibrium theory contains a strong conservative bias that favors the status quo among the current power elite.

Part I: The Politics of the Political Science Profession

In the 1960s, about a decade after Easton's criticisms of equilibrium theory in political science, a small group of insurgent political scientists began voicing similar and additional criticisms of the political science profession. They protested the lack of political science studies of important social issues, such as the expanding Vietnam War and numerous domestic injustices, like persistent poverty, class privilege, and racial discrimination. As members of the American Political Science Association (APSA), they demanded to know what usefulness organized political science has in a society in which the profession is irrelevant to the understanding and solving of social problems. They objected to the now overt, so-called "professional ethic" that required political scientists to strive to maintain a "value neutral" organization with little or no role in the policy making process of the United States. They felt the "ethical impulse" that Easton mentioned, and argued that political science, in their view, should play an active role in the political process by criticizing government activities and by proposing alternative policies and legislation to help resolve social problems and improve life for the people in the US and the rest of the world.

Some of these advocates for activism formed a group within the APSA. It came to be known as "the Caucus for a New Political Science" (CNPS).[4] Their questioning of the purposes of political science presented an existential challenge to the prevailing regime. They accused the regime of hypocrisy, because it pretended to be "scientifically neutral," when by their silence on social issues, they in fact allowed the problems to fester. Indeed, some prominent members of the APSA actually lent their expertise to the war propagating State Department.[5] The CNPS rejected the philosophical assumptions the APSA regime used to justify its pretenses. For example, as one historian of the CNPS movement, Clyde Barrow, says, "new political science rejects the fact-value distinction," and "seeks to bridge that dichotomy."[6]

The dichotomy was "bridged" by showing that the dominant positivistic behavioral paradigm is *in practice* an expression of an implicit conservative ideology. Barrow quotes one of the founders of the Caucus, Christian Bay, who criticized the lack of intellectual honesty of those "logical positivist behavioralists" who claim to have no "normative commitments."[7] Thus, both Easton and new political science writers saw that the merely verbal separation of fact and value collapses when actual practice is examined. In practice, believers in equilibrium theory acted as advocates for preserving the status quo.

Barrow reports that in opposition to this APSA establishment conservatism, the "new political science proposed an equally ideologically driven critique."[8] This critique would come from a more liberal-to-radical perspective, and would be authentically overt, rather than disingenuously covert. Indeed, beyond critique, these ideologically driven radical leaning political scientists would produce their own empirical studies in contrast to the more conservative positivistic pluralist writings.

CNPS member, Michael Parenti, for instance, started from a radical position when he took up the study of the American power structure. From this point of view he critiqued Robert Dahl's *Who Governs?* by exposing the implications of Dahl's "pluralism" as having a conservative bias.[9] The pluralists focused on organized groups of power elites as the only relevant players in the policy making process. Their writings neglected to acknowledge any political significance for the unorganized or less organized and less privileged outsiders. Those folks appeared to be merely the pawns of the powerful elites, and by implication without power of their own.

Parenti, and likeminded radical political scientists, went on to reverse the pluralist approach, and study power structures "from the bottom up." Despite their political philosophies and moral motivations, these new political scientists produced important and insightful studies which, in Barrow's view, had as much or more empirical validity as the works of the supposedly "value neutral" status quo supporting pluralists.[10]

The CNPS Political Efforts

The CNPS movement was, in effect, an effort to re-organize the political science profession. In the first ten years of its role as critic of APSA's covert conservativism, from 1969 to 1979, CNPS ran 10 candidates for APSA president, and several candidates for other Association positions. In their efforts to change the direction of the profession, they "pursued a vigorous organizational strategy within the APSA." However, while APSA offices can still be contested, since their last bid for high office, according to Barrow, CNPS members have generally been content with being a "loyal opposition."[12]

While he does not try to explain CNPS's campaign losses, one reason for losing those past elections may be that, as Barrow writes, there has never been "a consensus on what constitutes a new political science beyond its critical stance toward the existing discipline."[13] In other words, CNPS offered APSA members nothing positive to vote for, only a shared disaffection with the establishment. Thus, in the absence of a clear alternative, the "academic establishment – who reproduce themselves in official positions and dominate the Association's journals," control resources, have access to grant money, and hold positions of prestige and power, remain fully ensconced.[14]

Ignorance about Easton

Unfortunately, the writers in the CNPS movement were among those political scientists that John Gunnell referred to when he observed that, as we quoted in Chapter 1, David Easton's main work, *The Political*

System, "has now become somewhat a prisoner of the perspectives that have subsequently informed its interpretive history." He questions whether the book has ever been truly understood.[15]

Ten years before the emergence of the CNPS movement, Easton, as we have seen, criticized equilibrium theory in political science for often acting as "a concealed ethical premise." Making the same criticism, the CNPS writers did not credit Easton, perhaps because they hadn't read him. Like several political scientists at the time, they tended to lump Easton in with the "positivistic behavioralists" they criticized. Reflecting the widespread misunderstanding of Easton, Barrow writes:

> David Easton, who played a major role in initiating the behavioral revolution in political science ... proposed that scholars study a political system defined as 'those interactions through which values are authoritatively allocated for a society.' Such an analysis would focus on decision-making (i.e., authoritative allocation of values) and how these authoritative allocations facilitate *the equilibrium* of the overall social system.[16]

Of course, as we have seen, Easton rejected equilibrium theory after a lengthy analysis of its shortcomings in his major work, *The Political System*.[17] Thus, the "urban myth" of Easton as a proponent of equilibrium theory and supporter of the status quo has dragged on from then until now.[18]

The Easton-CNPS Areas of Agreement

Had they been better informed about Easton's critique of the profession, they would have been aware of his vision for an alternative way of organizing American political science. Easton had already dealt in his own way with many of the issues they raised. One of the key issues is that of the so-called "fact-value" distinction, and some of its variants. We have seen that the CNPS activists exposed the APSA elites pretense of "scientific neutrality" as being a cover for the actual practice of refraining from any critical engagement in politics. Pretending to only be concerned with "facts," the actual practice of these elites was in line with conservative values. So, like Easton, the CNPS writers recognized that, while distinguishable from a logical point of view, in practice there was no separation of "facts" and "values." Instead, the focus on facts was used as a cover for letting the status quo persist. In reaction, and perhaps overreaction, to this conservativism, the CNPS activists called for the APSA to openly practice leftist values.

Like the new political science writers, Easton understood that political philosophies, which are sets of value preferences, do play a role in political science. He frankly acknowledged "the impossibility for political research ever to free itself from involvement with values."[19] In his view, like that of many Caucus members, "the goal of value-free research is a myth, unattainable."[20]

Easton explicitly rejected the notion of, in his words, the claims of "morally neutral research" asserted by those behavioralists who subscribed, again in his words, to "the classical view of positivism."[21] This was long before Christian Bay said the same thing. While Easton regarded his views as being in a different category of "behavioralism" than the "positivists," this distinction has gone largely unrecognized in political science.[22]

Part II: Easton's Third Way

Contrary to positivistic myths and misconceptions, the fact-value distinction does not mean that political scientists must somehow conduct research and write about their findings without any values. That is nonsense. To be human is to be a valuer. Easton and the writers of new political science agree on that. But a simple "rejection of the fact-value distinction," as Barrow proclaimed, misses an opportunity for a more subtle understanding of the role of values in political science.

Easton recognized that values, including moral values, "not only provide the matrix which shapes the selection of an empirical problem for investigation, but they mold the formulation of the problem, the selection of data, and even their interpretation."[23] Writing in the 1950s, and citing supportive literature, Easton proclaimed that the "ideal of a value-free social science has revealed itself as a chimera."[24] In Easton's view, science cannot be conducted without values, which are the bases for all choices. However, he could not accept, as a model for the profession, either the covert conservativism of APSA elites, or the radicalism of the CNPS writers. Indeed, Easton offered what I will call a "Third Way" for organizing political science.[25]

The Process of Research

In his organizational plan, Easton distinguished between three *phases* of research in the conduct of empirical political science.[26] These are the input phase of research, which includes problem selection and formulation, the conduct of research, and the output of the results.

1. Subject Selection

First, in doing political science research, of course, a subject matter must be selected. This act in itself implies values. Values are the motivations for choices, and choices reflect the values behind them. Easton recognized that a political scientist's choice of a research topic is a personal matter. The study of a subject may be undertaken for numerous reasons, such as for pay, or out of intellectual curiosity, or to indulge some passion for or against a given policy or social condition made salient by one's political philosophy. For Easton, a distinction can be made between *moral values* and other types of values. Moral values are just one of the types of values that can go into the selection of a research project. In fact, rather than a single factor, a mix of values may be behind a choice of topics. However, there is no "scientific" way of subject matter selection. It is a personal choice.

Aside from the two *moral* positions of conservatives and radicals, Barrow notes that members of the Caucus were highly critical of those positivistic behavioralists who have, claiming to be scientific, "routinely selected research topics" simply because those topics suited their data collecting quantitative methodology. Besides the conservative policy implications, the results of that approach have often proven "trivial, narrow, and apolitical."[27] Easton's critique of "hyperfactualism," as mentioned in Chapter 1, is similar. Indeed, this is one of his reasons for devising his axiom, or rule of relevance.

As a norm, his rule of relevance asserts values about how political science choices "ought" to be made. For example, whatever one's motivation or political philosophy at the time of topic selection, topics selected *ought* to be related to the authoritative allocation of values for a society. But this is an example of *science values* rather than the moral values of some political philosophy. As a *procedural ought*, it is nevertheless an expression of values.[28] As we will discuss further below, this ought has no necessary preferences for either conservative or radical politics. And rather than eliminating such values, it curbs them. Easton's term "secondary criterion of selection" can be used to distinguish his rule of relevance from other, more secondary, values.[29]

Whether or not a researcher's motivation for topic selection should be disclosed is a matter for debate within the profession. Easton favored disclosure, especially of one's political philosophy.[30] But he recognized that there are issues to consider. Perhaps a researcher's political leanings or motivation are unconscious, and therefore he or she cannot disclose what they are. With that problem in mind, Easton recommended that political scientists study political philosophy for the sake of "moral self-clarification."[31]

So far, then, Easton's discussion clarifies the relationship between political philosophy and political science by acknowledging the role political philosophy can play at the point of selecting a research project. There is no inconsistency for Caucus members to want both to help make "a better world,"[32] and to apply the methods of science. As we have said, a nuanced understanding of values distinguishes between types of values, such as scientific values, moral values, and other values of personal interest. The very selection of a research topic shows that there can be no such thing as a value-free political science. Even if *moral* values do not play a part in the selection of a research topic, to make a selection is to affirm a set of values. No matter what values a researcher brings to the choice of a topic, curbing their influence with Easton's rule of relevance will keep the research relevant.

2. The Conduct of Research

In the second phase, conducting the research, numerous choices are involved. How much should be quantitative, and how much qualitative? A research project might include, for example, participant observation as well as statistics. Multiple research techniques are available to political scientists, so choices from among them are necessary.[33]

Often, more material is gathered than is necessary for reporting the results of research. So, what material is relevant to the report must be decided. And, not only what is to be reported, but, as Easton noted, the very language, or rhetorical style, of the report must be chosen. The personal characteristics of researchers, which includes their values, genius, skill, creativity, etc., are one reason why some studies stand out as more interesting and insightful than others.

3. Validating Output

While problems of verifying research results are not discussed in Barrow's history of the CNPS, their commitment to a radical political science implies that the "validity" of research results would depend on the acceptability of those results to their political point of view. This would make "political correctness" a standard for assessing the scientific acceptability of a study. But in Easton's view, the empirical validity of research results can be determined by *scientific standards*, and thus avoid the problem of a confirmation bias due to political preferences. In other words, while political philosophy can play a role in the selection of a research project, it need not have any role to play in validating the soundness of the results. Empirical validity, he writes, depends not on ideological values, but on assessments of how well research claims "correspond … to reality."[34] This correspondence is assessed, not by laboratory testing, but by the researcher's judgment and by peers who exercise their own "good reasoning" based on their own knowledge and observations, and who seek to determine whether the research results accord with their own professional experience. These are the elements in his conception of "a rigorous methodology that could produce knowledge of an intersubjectively valid sort."[35]

So, at the second stage of doing professional political science, i.e., assessing the empirical validity of research findings, moral judgments, in Easton's Third Way, are out of place, and the values of good science control the process. In other words, Easton's behavioralism permits philosophy at the input phase of research, a choice of mixed methods for the execution of the research, and scientific scrutiny, based on the values of science, at the output phase.[36]

Pure and Applied Research

Easton continues his discussion of the role of values in political science as he further distinguishes between pure and applied research, and both of these from their subject matter, the phenomenal, or ground level, of actual politics, or political behavior.[37] Only a brief summary of these concepts is necessary for this discussion.

Pure Research

For Easton, the two types of research, pure and applied, would be activities outside the realm of politics, but which examine that realm.[38] Pure research might be concerned with such matters as whether a given set of social interactions constitute a "political" function, or are something else. A Tupperware party, for example, can have the same overt appearance as a fund raiser for a candidate for public office. Both would have a group of people sitting in a living room, listening to a pitch, and then handing checks to the host. In an effort to classify this activity correctly, pure research could entail interviews of the participants after the event, or participant observation during the event. If it is a fund raiser, then following the money so as to describe how it is spent in the campaign, can also be matters of pure research.

Pure research can include surveys about the opinions held by the public, for instance, towards campaign financing. In the Eastonian context, then, pure research includes the description of behavior, and *interpreting* the mentation of actors (such as meanings and intentions) as to whether they acting in relation to the authoritative allocation of values.

Identifying and explaining the workings of demands, supports, the conversion process, and outputs in a particular political system are principal functions for pure research. Studying whether, and to what extent, political alienation exists among the members of a political system, and the impact this has on the system's legitimacy, would be a pure research project. "Basic research," writes Easton, means "Research without regard for its possible uses."[39]

Applied Research

Applied research in Easton's scheme can be understood as building on the descriptions and analyses of pure research, but with more focus on the stresses or problems found in the political system. Suppose opinion surveys reveal adverse attitudes towards campaign finance practices. Applied research could try to identify the more significant causes of these attitudes, and assess whether or not they constitute a serious threat to the political system. Proposing mechanisms for alleviating such adverse effects could be included in the study. Applied research might look into whether such reforms as public funding, or more regulation of contributions and spending, would reduce system stresses by alleviating public resentments toward current practices.[40]

If there is no, or very little, public resentment towards the way campaigns are being financed, then there would be little threat to the system. Then there would be less of a problem for applied researchers to take on in a professional role. However, the options for political scientists of taking political action outside of their professional roles will be discussed momentarily.

Easton's Critical Political Science

In Easton's political science, the problem solving orientation of applied political science does not necessarily favor perpetuating the status quo of a regime, or power elite. Suppose solid research shows that a "military industrial complex" exists, and that it is sustaining a policy output of perpetual war, for example by transitioning from Afghanistan to a proxy war in Ukraine. Suppose further that it can be shown that this part of the political system is serving its own interests at the expense of the whole by demanding resources which could have been used for improving social services such as by making health care and education free. By highlighting such harms to the system, and then suggesting a means for reversing this flow of resources, an applied political science study would actually threaten the interests of the dysfunctional military industrial complex, and not tend towards sustaining the status quo, or equilibrium, of power relations.

Or suppose an applied research project, studying the US political system, showed that both voter turnout (as an input phase) and Congressional responses to voter demands (output phase) would improve under a system of public financing. This would not be a confirmation of the status quo, but would reveal inconsistencies between the political self-image of Americans, as living in a "democracy," and the actual practice of elites. Hypotheses as to how to improve this condition would be well within the scope of applied political science.

Political Behavior and Political Science

The examples of a campaign finance study and a foreign policy study can also be considered to highlight the difference between applied political science and ground level political advocacy. One difference between science and activism, for example, is the audience being addressed. A political scientist's audience depends upon which kind of work he or she chooses to do. If a project is pure or applied research, the audience will be different than if the choice is to advocate a particular policy. Applied research is addressed to other professionals. This can include government professionals as well as political science colleagues. The language used would be technical and emotionally detached.

The language of policy advocacy is of a different sort. It is designed to stimulate action and perhaps arouse emotions. It is aimed at a broader audience, such as party leaders, policy activists, and the attentive public. Editors of professional journals, as well as their readership, generally have a sharp eye for the difference between the language of applied research writings and that of policy advocacy. The moral impulse of policy advocates will likely lead them to publish in the more popular political publications. Only that which is offered to professional journals for publication, or appears in books as the product of professional research, is required to pass scientific muster. Thus, the line between applied political science and policy advocacy can be policed by professional journal editors, peer reviewers, as well as colleagues.

Applied studies are not always divorced from practical politics. Suppose a campaign finance study or a foreign policy study is addressed to professionals in an applied political science journal. These studies can also provide solid empirical evidence which political activists could use in support of whatever positions they want to advocate in the political process. If the methods used and the results obtained have passed muster in the community of peers, activists can use the knowledge to their own ends without being vulnerable to attacks on the validity of their facts and solutions.

Of course, political scientists are also members of a political system, and are not obliged to keep their opinions to themselves.[41] Easton's distinctions would not preclude CNPS members, or any other subgroup of the profession, from being "scholar activists" within the political process. Besides being a journalist or a politician, a political scientist can be a public intellectual. "Conservatives have understood this fact better than radicals and leftists," writes Barrow.[42] He sees "conservative public intellectuals" as a model for activists on the left. But in Easton's political science, by engaging in such activity, a political scientist would necessarily cross a logical line and descend from the "professional" realm of science into the wild world of politics. Indeed, the distinction between applied political science and political advocacy draws a clear line between *professional* and *personal* activity for a political scientist.

The Radical Objection

Of course, not all political scientists will accept Easton's scheme. Consider this quote of Barrow who observes that "What makes the new political science a radical political science is the nature of the social problems it identifies and the solutions that it proposes for those problems."[43] This statement neglects the three levels of political science that Easton proposes, and simply connects all political science research directly with public policy advocacy. The line between professional and personal activity disappears. Barrow, it seems, would have all Caucus members act as public intellectuals, think tank operators, or party platform researchers who identify a social or political problem, and then advocate a radical policy for resolving the issue. Those are legitimate activities, but following Easton's organizational plan, those activities would not be "political science." They would be a part of the political process. The audience would not be colleagues within the political science profession, but political activists, party leaders, or public officials (persons of a different profession).[44]

However, in Easton's view, there *can* be a "radical political science." For example, when, in Barrow's words, "the nature of the social problems it identifies" are deliberately selected from a radical point of view. Such project selection is well within the scope of professional political science research. The proviso is that, to remain professional, "the solutions that it proposes" would be framed as applied political science, and addressed to an audience of professional peers, rather than to a popular audience. This would indeed be a "new political science" because political philosophies of all sorts, from radical to moderate to conservative, would have an acknowledged role in the problem selection stage of research. Thus, there can be a "socialist behavioralism," which would select problems from a socialist point of view, and then conduct the research with those behavioral methods which are appropriate for the project. The research results would be subject to peer criticism. To merit inclusion in the category "political science," the research results, whether pure or applied, would be related to the authoritative allocation of values, and addressed to peers rather than the public. Validation would depend, not on how well the proposals fit the socialist program, but on how peers applied the scientific standards of validation.[45]

APSA Article II

Although policy advocacy is not within the province of political science, there is a role for the American Political Science Association to play in practical politics. As distinct from moral values, the political science profession, speaking through the APSA, can advocate what could be called the "values of scientific methodology."

For political science to fulfil its mission to study the political system in all its aspects, certain political conditions must be met in actual political systems. If political scientists conducting ethnographic research are compelled to be accompanied by "minders," for example, their participant observations, personal interviews, and focus group research will be so constrained and the results so unreliable as to be useless. If the members of a political system are so fearful of secret police and informers among their neighbors, even if there are no minders present, the responses they give to political science researchers will also be worthless as factual material for such studies as those which probe public opinion and regime legitimacy. Likewise, if government officials are too afraid to speak openly, how reliable would interviews of them be? Just as there are countries that are unsafe for journalists, so there are such countries in which political science cannot be freely conducted. These countries could be identified, and official APSA advocacy that they be more open could be publicized. The APSA could lobby the US government at a variety of points to put pressure on those countries to open up for political science research.

Advocacy of these scientific method values would not violate Article II of the APSA constitution. That Article states, in part, the APSA "will not commit its members on questions of public policy."[46] But criticizing governments on the basis of the profession's methodological needs is different in kind from asserting positions on questions of general public policy. Article II also states that the APSA will refrain from taking "positions not immediately concerned with its direct purpose [which is] to encourage the study of Political Science."[47] Demanding that governments provide conditions within which political science can do its work, and calling out those countries that do not provide the necessary conditions, falls squarely within the ambit of that "direct purpose" clause.

Also, one might question the logical consistency of the APSA proclaiming such a noble position as its "direct purpose to encourage the study of Political Science," while at the same time denying to the world free and open access to its journals. APSA is a tax free (501c3) organization, whose members lobby for and receive grants of tax payer money. Many of its prominent members, researchers, and officials are employed by public universities. So they are paid with tax payer funds to do the work of political science. Even professors at private universities are paid for the teaching and research they do. Should scholars from poor countries, and students on tight budgets be required to pay for the privilege of reading articles already paid for by taxes?

Also, Open Access is essential if the aim of producing reliable knowledge is to be fully realized. Easton asked, how can we "transcend our own cultural and methodological bias"?[48] For example, if the work of those political scientists from industrialized Western nations is only screened for bias by fellow well-off Westerners, then parochial slants may not be detected. Open Access journals would enable and encourage political scientists from all sorts of underprivileged cultures and classes to participate in the validation of published research findings. This openness would greatly advance the APSA's "direct purpose to encourage the study of Political Science."

The Place of Political Philosophy in Political Science

In *The Tragedy of Political Science*, David Ricci laments what he sees as the long and thus far failed effort of the discipline to reconcile the conflict between the pro-science and the pro-philosophy parts of the profession. With no unifying paradigm to bring these factions together, Ricci warns that the profession will continue drifting down a path of increasing fragmentation, as more divisions, caucuses, and areas of specialty are constructed.[49]

However, as we have seen, in Easton's organizational design there is a distinct place for political philosophy in the political science profession. This is primarily at the subject selection phase of research. As we have indicated, political scientists can chose to undertake a research project for a number of reasons, political philosophy included. Thus, the study of political philosophy has an important place in the political science curriculum, for example, as Easton suggested, as an aid in moral self-clarification. Of course, political philosophy can also play a prominent role in political practice. Political parties and other political groups, like public interest groups, organize around the shared political philosophy of their members. Each group hopes to shape public policy to suit its own philosophical principles.

The tasks of the two fields, science and philosophy, have some significant differences. By focusing its study on the political system, political science can do several things. It can correct misconceptions, and deepen understanding, about how political systems function. It can assess how well a system is operating. And it can diagnose what causes dysfunction, and propose remedies. But political science cannot answer philosophical questions such as "what is justice," or "what is the good society?," or "what is freedom?," or "how ought people behave?," or "what is the good life?," not to mention "what is the meaning of life?." The questions of political philosophy, and of philosophy in general, are a part of human life, and will surely spur debate and disputes for a long time to come, both inside and outside of the political science profession.

Far from being the "end of political philosophy," as some positivists might think, it is an essential element in Normative Political Science. In the relationship of political philosophy and political science, the latter is like the books between matching bookends. There is political philosophy at the start of political science research, and, in the political arena, political philosophy at the end of political science research, with pure and applied science in between. Indeed, one of the characteristics of human beings that distinguishes them from even the most intelligent of animals is our unending creation of moral philosophies and political ideals. This oddity of nature is likely to persist for a long time into our future. Easton's political science fully accommodates this peculiarity of humanity.

Conclusion: The Normative Political Science Alternative

Normative Political Science, unlike the CNPS movement, offers political science a fully developed alternative paradigm to that of the positivistic status quo.[50] The Easton-Hartman Synthesis fits right in with Easton's vision for the organization of the profession. Both empirical and evaluative political science are distinct from political practice. The assessment of a political system's operational goodness is an option in the realm of pure research. For example, applying performance measures as to how efficiently and effectively parts of the system, such as agencies, are operating would also be a pure research project.

Applied research could discuss, or offer, proposals as to how an agency might improve its performance. Lessons could be learned from comparative studies of similar agencies in different political systems, whether foreign countries or other states in the USA. Such suggestions would, of course, be theoretical exercises addressed to professional colleagues. Whether or not political activists would be inspired to advocate the implementation of the proposals of applied political science is a matter outside of the profession's concerns and boundary lines.

Public opinion research also has pure and applied dimensions. These will be discussed in the following chapter, the book's Conclusion.

Endnotes

1. Easton 1953, 1971, 223. Easton uses the terms "moral" and "ethical" as interchangeable. Political science historian, John Gunnell, observes that the "idea of an empirical theory of politics was always conceived of as part of a program for intervening in political life." In Monroe, ed. 1997, at 47f. Indeed, his discussion in Monroe, Chapter Two, sets the historical stage for the introduction of the Normative Political Science paradigm. The instant book offers a vision of the relationship between political science and politics that can be readily institutionalized, as the founders of the APSA had hoped.

2. Ibid., pp. 298-299.

3. Ibid., pp. 299-302. This use of equilibrium "usually reflects the democratic ethos," 299.

4. After 60 years of using that name, the members of the Caucus decided to change their name to "the Caucus for a Critical Political Science." See Clyde Barrow 2022.

5. Barrow writes that "many of the profession's top academic elites, including the APSA's executive director, were actually discovered to have ties to the CIA." Barrow 2008, at 234f. In confirmation of Barrow's claim, I found that during the 1967 APSA annual meeting the news broke out that "Evron M. Kirkpatrick, the APSA's executive director, and Max M. Kampelman, the treasurer, were then … president and vice-president of OPR," Operations and Policy Research, Inc., which had received CIA financial support. An APSA investigation concluded that they "were not involved in a conflict of interest, and that they should, in fact, be commended for their long service to the association." The report candidly concluded that, "Not everyone was satisfied with this outcome." Robert J. Samuelson. "Political Science: CIA, Ethics Stir Otherwise Placid Convention." Science New Series, Vol. 157, No. 3795 (Sep. 22, 1967), pp. 1414-1417

6. Barrow 2008, 244.

7. Ibid., 220.

8. Ibid., 235.

9. Ibid., 230. See Michael Parenti, *Democracy for the Few* (1974).

10. Ibid., 231. Howard Zinn's well known work, *A People's History of the United States* (1980), was written in the same spirit that animated the CNPS, although he was a historian rather than a political scientist.

11. Ibid., 237.

[12.] Ibid., 224.

[13.] Ibid., 216.

[14.] Ibid., 241, 233. Considering the 10 unsuccessful tries for the APSA presidency, Barrow's comment that "capturing the APSA was never crucial to either the political or intellectual objectives of new political science" seems to be an expression of "the Loser's Excuse" rather than a thought through explanation of their losses.

[15.] Gunnel 2013, 198.

[16.] Barrow 2008, 217. Emp. add.

[17.] See discussion in this book's Chapter 1. Also, Easton 1953, 1971, 266f; esp. 299f.

[18.] In an obituary, meant to be favorable, Luigi Graziano writes, "Behaviouralism focused primarily on mass phenomena and conceived political equilibrium as the result of social forces." Graziano, Luigi. "David Easton (1917–2014)." Eur Poli Sci 13, 323–326 (2014). https://doi.org/10.1057/eps.2014.21 Cf. another obituary without reference to "equilibrium" at,

https://www.encyclopedia.com/social-sciences/applied-and-social-sciences-magazines/easton-david

Also see the discussion of equilibrium theory in this book's Chapter 1, and the references therein to contemporary misunderstandings of Easton.

[19.] Easton 1953, 1971, 223.

[20.] Ibid.

[21.] Ibid., 224.

[22.] Easton may be partly to blame for the confusion. In one of his books he published what he called the "Behavioralist's Credo." In doing this, he saw himself as making an "alliance" with other behavioralists so that their views could prevail over the dominant "hyperfactualism" in his day. See his discussion of these paradigm politics in 1965a, Chapter One.

[23.] Easton 1953, 1971, 225.

[24.] Ibid.

[25.] As President of the APSA, Easton gave his Presidential Address at the 1969 annual meeting of the Association. (It is appended to the second edition of *The Political System*, and my page citations refer to that.) In the speech, he observed that the "behavioralism" which he had helped to introduce, has become, at least in the United States, "the dominant approach in the last decade." (327) Without referring to the CNPS by name, Easton acknowledges all of their criticisms which we mention in the text. He announces that these criticisms constitute a "Post-Behavioral Revolution." (323) He admits that the newly dominant behavioralism has failed to overcome the problem of "value neutrality" resulting in an a-critical stance towards government policy and action. He is sympathetic towards the "post behavioral revolution" demand for a political science that can "prescribe." (329) That is, offer principles for criticizing policies and make suggestions for how to improve social conditions.

He regrets that "we do not yet have … this kind of organization." (346) He concedes to the critics that "our discipline needs reordering." (341) He then engages in a sustained effort at what he calls "creative speculation," or brainstorming, on issues that range from reforming the university (356) to the problem of how to reorganize the political science profession so as to satisfy the legitimate demands of the dissenters.

Echoing much of what he wrote in the 1950s on these issues, Easton discusses how he envisions the primary challenges to the profession's behavioral paradigm and to the profession's role as an institution in society. He agrees that the positivistic "Fact-Value" distinction turns out to be hypocritical in practice. How can the profession that specializes in the study of politics and government have nothing to offer for bringing peace where there is war, and for relieving the sufferings caused by economic deprivation and injustice?

In the course of his creative speculations in the speech, Easton is most concerned with clarifying the relationships between political science and political philosophy. More specifically, he wants to lay out the right relationships between, what are for him, the most important constituent elements in "the division of labor" for political science. These are pure (or basic) research, applied research, political philosophy, and the participation of political scientists in the political process. (While, of course, teaching political science is a major task for the profession, it is not essential to Easton's discussion.) The suggestions Easton made in the 1969 speech, as I said, are like those offered in *The Political System* from several years earlier, and, taken together, are crystallized in this chapter.

[26] Evaluative political science will be discussed further below.

[27] Barrow 2008, 221.

[28] Cf. Easton 1953, 1971, 78f. As we saw in the Introduction to this book, Robert Merton makes it clear that science has its own values. These include the

norms for the professional organization, as well as methodological norms. Easton was likely influenced by Merton's writings, as he cites these throughout the text.

[29] Easton 1953, 1971, 370-371.

[30] Ibid., 228.

[31] Ibid., 228-229f. Easton returned to this theme in his 1969 APSA Presidential Address. See pp. 340-341 passim.

[32] Barrow 2008, 215.

[33] The practice of using such mixed methods has a long history in political science running from Charles Merriam, who wrote in the early twentieth century, to

Matthew Desmond, an early twenty-first century writer. RE: Merriam's use of mixed methods, such as statistics and personal observation, see Crick 1959, 133f; Tanenhaus and Somit 1967, 87f; Ricci 1984, 77f. Desmond 2016 used a mixed methods approach similar to Merriam. His methods are discussed in numerous footnotes throughout the text. Two reviews of Desmond worth comparing are Schram 2016 and Kelleher 2016.

34. Easton 1953, 1971, 225- 226 passim.

35. Quote re "good reasoning" at Ibid., 226. Quote re "intersubjectively valid" at Ibid., 377. A similar "correspondence theory" applies when assessing the goodness of the operational functions of a political system. The more a function "corresponds" with the ideal set for it in the theory of the political system, the better it is.

36. Insofar as the validation of research findings is based on the intersubjective agreement of peers, it is a community enterprise. As such, the process may not always be as "pure" as the ideal of science might suggest. For example, the factual dispute over whether the American power structure is democratically pluralistic or undemocratically elitist may not be easily resolved by mere empirical evidence. It may be that a Kuhnian analysis must be brought in at this point. If the pluralist view is clear from within the covertly conservative positivistic behavioral paradigm, and the elitist view is clear from within the values permitted, mixed methods CNPS paradigm, then the resolution to the conflict may have to be political. That, in turn, could involve the control of the APSA. Paradigm politics will be discussed further below.

37. Easton 1953, 1971, 81-89f, and 350f. And see Chapter 3 herein.

38. As noted above, in a Kuhnian analysis, scientific knowledge is never outside the realm of paradigm competition, or "politics" in an informal sense, because paradigms are ultimately chosen as a result of political competition. Even the distinction between pure and applied political research is paradigm related, and was not widely used prior to the "Behavioral Revolution." Easton, id. 78f. So Easton's distinctions between three levels for political science assumes a condition of what Kuhn calls "normal science." In other words, Easton's scheme is a social construct which can only be made a reality by the personal commitment to it by a critical mass of political scientists who then make their new perspective mainstream through collective action. See, Thomas Kuhn, *The Structure of Scientific Revolutions* (University of Chicago Press, 1962, second edition 1970).

39. Easton 1953, 1971, 376.

40. Towards the conclusion of his 1985 article on the "four stages" in the history of political science, Easton seemed to still be defensive after the "Post Behavioral Revolution," which challenged, among other things, his earlier distinction

between pure and applied research. (See Easton 1985.) His notion of pure research as primary in science did not seem to be catching on among those who wanted more problem tackling research.

But the Easton-Hartman Synthesis puts the issue into a new perspective. One of its virtues is to reinforce the validity of some of the very concepts about which he was becoming less sure. Using the theory of the political system as a standard for assessing the performance of a behavioral political system sheds a laser-like light on those areas where applied knowledge and research are required to bring a system up to par. Thus, scientific theory provides standards by which to both identify problems in a political system and by which to select problems for applied research. Of course, researchers remain free to select research projects for any reason, as we discussed in the text. If Easton had known about the Hartman-Easton Synthesis, he might have used that to mark the "fifth stage" in the development of American political science; i.e., the one presented here.

[41.] Except for the ethical obligation of teachers to refrain from partisan advocacy in the classroom. See Easton 1953, 1971, 358f. Of course, the values of a particular political philosophy are implicated in the choices made for teaching curricula. Somit and Tanenhaus write of "the profession's continued commitment to education for democratic citizenship." Somit and Tanenhaus *The Development of Political Science*, ibid., 171f. However, the instant article is concerned only with the research aspects of political science.

[42.] Barrow 2008, 242.

[43.] Ibid., 243.

[44.] A search of the term "public intellectual" produced over 24,000,000 links. Among them, a 2005 poll which placed Noam Chomsky as the most highly rated public intellectual out of 100 mentioned.
https://www.infoplease.com/culture-entertainment/prospectfp-top-100-public-intellectuals

[45.] In positivist theory, testing predictions is the key to an "objective" validation, or verification. While that chimera has no place in Normative Political Science, as a practical matter, the remedial suggestions made by applied political scientists are forms of prediction, and implementation is their test. Similar ideas have been expressed. For example, "Traditional theories of politics, which show how government power can be used to serve the public interest, can be quantified and tested as empirical theory." See Miller, Trudy. "Normative Political Science." Review of Policy Research Vol. 9, Issue 2 December 1989. 232-246.

[46.] APSA Constitution, as amended on November 3, 2011 at,
https://www.apsanet.org/portals/54/Files/APASConstitution2011.pdf

[47.] Ibid.

[48.] Easton 1953, 1971, 340; quote from 1969 Address.

[49.] Ricci 1978. Unfortunately, Ricci re-states the standard misrepresentation of Easton's position on the concept of "equilibrium," at p.254. Indeed, in one of the pages Ricci cites in support of his claim, Easton actually calls the use of equilibrium theory to measure amounts of political power nothing more than "a pleasant intellectual game." Easton 1953, 1971 p.288-289.

[50.] Perhaps this complete alternative paradigm could provide the campaign advantage in APSA politics that the losing CNPS campaigners lacked.

Conclusion:

Diagnosis and Causation in Normative Political Science

Part One: A Review of Pure and Applied Research

As we have seen, Easton divides the labor of political science into the two pursuits of pure and applied research. This division of labor calls attention to two methodological factors which Easton did not fully address, diagnosis and causal theory. We will discuss these after a brief re-cap of the practices of pure and applied research.

Pure research is primarily descriptive. That is, the operations of a system under study, either as a whole, or any of its parts, are observed and described. The meanings political actors act upon are interpreted and recorded. Normative Political Science adds an evaluative process to that empirical approach. That is, the performance of the system, or any of its parts, once its operations have been described, is then assessed under the standards established by Easton's definition of the political system. This assessment will reveal functions of the system that are performing well or poorly, and can assess the degree to which the performance is above or under par.

Another dimension of pure research is the study of public opinion. The results of this research will show the degrees to which the public is supportive, non-supportive, or even hostile towards the system, or any of its operations. This, too, is a form of description.

Of course, in either the case of low performance evaluations or of problematic public opinion, the next practical step is to diagnose the causes of the shortcomings. But before discussing the nature and technique of diagnosis, a word or two must be said about applied research, the other half in Easton's division of labor.

Applied research builds upon the findings of pure research. For example, suppose subpar areas in system performance and/or public opinion have been described in pure research studies, and no effort at diagnosing causes has been tendered. Applied research can undertake an original diagnosis of the problems, and then propose hypothetical remedies for these problems. If pure research studies have diagnosed the causes of troublesome areas, applied research can accept these conclusions, or criticize, or add to the proposed causes given in the pure research literature. Suggested remedies can then be put forward. Proposed remedies can also be the subject of criticism or refinement in succeeding articles published in professional journals.

Applied research might consider which of all the stresses on a system are most tolerable, or are most likely to disrupt public order, or even threaten the existence of the system. Of course, the rhetoric of applied research articles should be policed for professionalism by editors and peer reviewers. Political activists will follow this literature and take from it what they will.

Thus, diagnosing the causes of below par performances, or of public dissatisfaction, can be undertaken in the course of either pure or applied research. Just as the selection of research projects is up to the researcher, so she or he can decide whether or not to try their hand at diagnosing the causes of problems, or, in pure research, just leave off at the descriptions of them. Whether for diagnosis or proposing remedies, causation is central. Therefore, a clear conception of causation is required. We will offer that in this Conclusion.

Part Two: What is Diagnosis in Normative Political Science?

Diagnosis, as the term is used here, is the effort to find the causes of either subpar performance, or of dissatisfied public opinion. The methods for assessing political system performance and for discovering public opinion have been discussed in prior chapters, particularly Chapters 1, 3, and 5. Once the dysfunctional conditions for either have been described, the causes of these conditions can be sought. As we will now see, each of these two types of factual conditions, system performance and public opinion, requires its own distinct theory of causation.

Extrinsic Causal Theory – for Low Performance Ratings

Low performance ratings can be probed to identify the causes in the operations of the system. The causes of low performance ratings will generally be of a very practical type. For example, if information is not flowing smoothly from input into the conversion process, the cause will likely be found in the performances of the relevant actors. Suppose public demands for cleaner air and water are not being converted into the legislation needed to produce those results. Upon a diagnosis of the causes of the inaction, it might be found that pressure groups related to the fossil fuel industries are compelling the law makers who are indebted to them to refrain from taking the action called for by their constituents. Other contributing causes could include the inability of law makers to reach an agreement, not due to outside pressure, but because of personal rivalries, or because of sheer indecisiveness, or some other factors.

Other explanations of a practical sort could be that the system lacks the resources to enforce the laws made in response to public input. Performances, of course, are actions, and the success or failure of actions is generally a practical matter involving skill, will, luck, and resources.

Intrinsic Causal Theory – for Public Sentience

The causal theory for diagnosing dissatisfied public opinion is different and more subtle than that for diagnosing low performance ratings. Understanding the political behavior of people is different than understanding political system operations. The nature of causation is different for each. As we have seen, malfunctioning parts in a system, such as corrupt officials, can be replaced, and this might correct the problem of poor performance. But when the problem is one of political unhappiness, different variables come into play.

Suppose, for example, the public has a vague and general sense of resentment and unhappiness with their government. One rule of thumb for understanding public discontent is that prior to disappointment there was an expectation. Disappointment generally results from events failing to satisfy the expectations people had for them. So, for diagnosing unsupportive or hostile feelings toward a system, or some part thereof, ascertaining the expectations of the people involved can be helpful. This can help to pin-point the cause of their feelings. Also, the political scientist might want to know why the people have the expectations they do. Perhaps politicians promised something they could not deliver. Every situation will probably be different, unique.

In diagnosing the displeasure of the public it might be helpful to consider whether or not their expectations were realistic. If the expectations were realistic, then perhaps something in the operation of the system was the cause of their disappointment. If the expectations were not realistic, then the system is not to blame for the disappointment of the people, but their own thinking is the cause of their frustration. We will return to this possibility in a moment.

Precision

As we have seen, Normative Political Science goes beyond merely descriptive practices and offers standards by which to assess how well a system is operating. When some, or all, of a system's functions are operating below par, Normative Political Science enables the political scientist to conduct precise diagnoses of the dysfunctions.

With Easton's theoretical separation of the dynamic political system into five distinct phases, that is, input, conversion, output, feedback, and the environment of the system, the researcher is provided with five interpretive frameworks through which he or she can focus her or his attention. This enables the researcher to assess the operation of each function, or the system as a whole. The study of operational dysfunction can lead to new insights and understanding as knowledge of each function accumulates. As Easton's Flow Chart suggests, his theory also enables the researcher to trace the effects of one set of dysfunctions on other parts of the system.

Easton's theoretical categories can also help the researcher with the diagnosis of public opinion. Suppose that general feelings of distrust, disapproval, or hostility are found in surveys, ethnography, or by other methods. Where the causes of such feelings are not obvious, or articulated by membership, an examination of each of the five system functions in relation to such feelings could reveal otherwise hard to understand connections. Once these causes have been identified, remedies to alleviate harms, or reduce hostilities, can be offered. From these insights lessons can be learned for how a regime could enhance the public's authentic satisfaction with their political system, if the regime so chooses.

As we have suggested, Normative Political Science incorporates the methods of interpretive political science. These methods are oriented to an empirical approach to the study of political behavior. Interpretive political science assumes, to a large extent, that political actors are acting upon the meanings in their minds. Indeed, Easton often refers to the theory of "the definition of the situation" as important to his understanding of political behavior.[1]

Thus, one aim of interpretation is to understand what meanings political actors are actually acting upon. In addition, interpretation seeks to understand what meanings particular operations of a political system have for its members. This approach also involves assumptions about the causal relations between system operations and the meanings these may have for the membership.

In the interpretive theory of causation, the people are not always the passive recipients of some outside causal factor making them unhappy. The people can play an active part in their own unhappiness. That is, the subject may not be just a passive recipient of the causal object, but play a more active role. As we have said, generally, the members of a system have expectations for its performance. Each person shapes and holds her or his own sets of expectations formed from the cues of society, socialization, education, the media, or their own information seeking and thought processes. Their expectations can be held with varying degrees of consciousness. Poor performance, or government acts inconsistent with these expectations, will likely result in the affected people feeling disappointment and other related feelings of non-support or hostility to their regime.

This theory of causation is not linear, as in positivistic theories of one billiard ball striking another and thus causing it to move. This theory is not a stimulus-response model, but much more interactive. Those mechanistic theories of causation cast the subject of the causal object in a passive role. But a more realistic model of political attitude formation rejects, at least in some ways, the attribution of passivity.[2] For example, the members of a political system will *interpret* the actions of their regime. Interpretations are mental activities. Suppose the members of a system interpret the action of the system's regime in a very negative way. To the extent that interpretation is an act of meaning creation, these members of a system have made the meanings that make them unhappy.

Thus when diagnosing dissatisfaction, the political scientist will be making an interpretation of interpretations. One question then arises, were the interpretations of the displeased people accurate or off base? Whether causes are system induced or self-created are variables for political scientists to consider especially when endeavoring to propose possible remedies for public discontent. Of course, the peers of a political scientist will pass judgment as to how accurate or inaccurate were his or her interpretations of the interpretations of the folks under study.[3]

Suppose a person dies after being shot. In this case a causal explanation assuming the passivity of the victim would probably be appropriate. The bullet killed the person, and he or she had no active part in bringing about that result. Mechanically, A (the bullet puncturing the heart) caused B (the demise of the victim). But in the interpretive theory of causation both subject and object can play an active part.

Suppose, for example, that research shows that Congress is unresponsive to public demands for more effective gun control. Some people see this inaction and feel frustrated, unheard, perhaps disrespected, or alienated. Are these feelings a mechanical result of the government inaction, a one way causation? Not for interpretive theory.

Why? Because the inaction of the government is *interpreted* in ways that generate their political unhappiness. This interpretation is a form of participation in the process. These interpretations were freely self-made, and those folks could have done otherwise.[4]

Do Self-Created Meanings have Limits?

Does the interpretive point of view assume that the powers of interpretation the people have are so independent of circumstance that even in the midst of violent suppression by a government the victims can interpret their conditions in ways that will have them feeling Bliss Consciousness? Not likely. (Not for sane people, anyway.) This interpretive theory assumes the people are relatively rational.

Interpretation is not just making stuff up. But for the acts of the regime, the people would not likely feel as they do. An output, for example, can be disappointing because the people expected something else. Perhaps they expected their government to do better than that.

While not caused mechanically, government actions can *prompt* a reaction among the public. This may be spoken of as a "caused interpretation."[5] Even without prompting, people can have *an intuitive sense* for how well their political system is operating. Poor operation can be something they sense and feel critical of, but without being able to pin point the cause of their critical feelings.

Nonmechanical causal relationships will vary in time and place, or circumstance. In another time and place, the meanings of government actions may be interpreted differently than they would be now. At one time, in Europe, frequent public floggings and hangings were a cause for celebration. Whole families might turn out and have a picnic while watching the festivities. In contemporary America, contrary to its Puritan past, such government behavior would likely be interpreted as outrageous oppression and intolerable abuse. Thus, causal explanations in interpretive political science must consider the cultural context if they are to correspond to the realities on the ground. Clearly, the complex mutual causal relation between government performance and public feeling remains an area well worth more research and analysis.

Remedies Should Fit the Problem

To the extent, if any, that the people are responsible for their own frustration, the nature of the remedies proposed by the applied political scientist will have to fit the situation. When interpretations are misguided or unrealistic, re-education might be required. There is surely no one-size-fits-all principle for finding and proposing remedies in applied political science. When a system's poor performance is clearly the cause of the public's displeasure, then the remedies must be sought in the system's operations.

As we mentioned, in Chapter Three, the authenticity of public responses to researchers, especially when asking respondents to rate government performance, should always be considered when interpreting the results of public opinion research. Respondents may not be authentic out of fear of reprisals from authorities, or may be people pleasing, or tell lies for other reasons. Remedies based on inauthentic responses risk being ineffective.

The Anchor in Reality

The interpretive approach lacks the imaginary anchor in "objective" knowledge with which the positivists delude themselves. The anchor in reality for interpretivists is the confidence in their methods, and the trust in the judgment of their peers, upon which consensus is based. Truth and goodness are what the members of the profession determine for themselves. Hypothetically, even a widely shared consensus of the profession could be mistaken. This is what Polanyi calls "the hazard of knowing." In his view, there is no way to escape such risk and responsibility.[6]

Principles of Diagnosis for Normative Political Science

- Diagnosis always follows the description of factual conditions.
- Diagnosis presupposes causation.
- Diagnosis entails tracing back likely causes to their origins, if possible.
- Diagnosis is required to explain the causes of below par performances that have been described.
- There is nothing to diagnose when a system works as expected. When a system is working well, the reason will generally be that the participants are acting correctly, that is, as required to sustain the smooth operation of a political system. Their correct actions can be described, but causal explanations are only needed for operational defects.
- Thus, for the clarity of explanatory political science, the "reasons" for success will be distinguished from the "causes" of failure.[7]

Heuristic Implications

The causal theory offered here has numerous heuristic implications for political science research. Among these implications is that the negative feelings of the people are probably *the symptom* of system dysfunction. These symptoms can be diagnosed by political scientists so as to discover their causes. Where public opinion is more satisfied and supportive, the reasons will likely be in the good performance of the system.

In conclusion, besides enabling the measurement of system performance, the Normative Political Science paradigm can be used as a diagnostic tool. That is, it can be used as a framework for identifying, and probing the causes of, dysfunction in a political system and discontent in the membership. Because this paradigm offers a conceptual framework that facilitates diagnosis in all the ways we have mentioned, we think it is an exciting new way to do research in political science. To further exemplify this approach, we will now turn to two examples of the complex causal relationships between system performance and public sentience. One for positive public sentience, the other for negative, indeed hostile, feeling.

Part Three: Two Examples of System Performance and the Resulting Public Sentience – China and Peru

The non-mechanistic theory of causation offered here will be illustrated, and perhaps tested, by the actual events of China and Peru. These political system specimens can be read with the following Propositions, or hypotheses, in mind :

- The operation of a political system will probably have a causal effect on the political sentience of the public.
- A well-functioning political system will probably engender high approval ratings among its membership.
- Likewise, a poorly functioning system will probably produce low approval ratings.

China

As we saw in Chapter Four, over the past 40 years the Chinese political system has helped lift nearly 800M people out of extreme poverty and into a new middle class. These people are as well off as any middle class in the Western world. As we have seen, the policy of "Common Prosperity" aims at sharing the wealth among the entire population. If they stay on that path their quality of life may soon exceed that of all Western nations.[8]

The extraordinarily successful operation of the Chinese political system is reflected in the pre-COVID approval ratings, which as we have seen were in the 90s for the national government. These two key variables – system performance and public ratings – are probably not in a mere relationship of concurrency, but more likely connected. That is, as we have said, the experience the people have had with the exceptional performance of the system is most likely their primary *reason* for giving the system these unusually high approval ratings.

Peru

The case of Peru provides quite a contrast with that of China. Recently there have been mass demonstrations and political violence in Peru. This case can be interpreted to lend credence to the causal principle that poor governing in a political system can cause corresponding low approval (and high disapproval) ratings.

In early December 2022, hundreds of "campesinos," that is the rural peasantry and indigenous people of Peru, flooded the capital, Lima, and other urban areas, in bus loads. Along with likeminded urban dwellers, they protested during the day and into the night. Their protests soon resulted in fatalities. Just in the first few days, over 50 Peruvian demonstrators were killed, most in violent clashes with the police. At least one police officer was also killed.[9]

Could the poor performance of the political system in Peru have been the cause of the rage which drove this rebellious action and the consequent tragic deaths? If so, how?

First, consider the environment in which the political system was operating. Nearly one in three citizens were then living in poverty; and that is still the case. While this includes millions of urban residents, "it is at its most intense in rural areas, where many still live without potable water, electricity, or access to public health care."[10]

Unfortunately, health care is so unavailable to so many Peruvians that, according to the Johns Hopkins University, Peru had the highest COVID-19 case-fatality ratio in the world, 4.9% as of February 4, 2023.[11] Also, the United Nations Food and Agriculture Organization has found that half of all

Peruvians are food insecure.[12]

According to a report in Foreign Policy magazine, 60% of Peruvians see their legislature as self-serving and corrupt.[13] Resentment is exacerbated by what Peruvians see as the corruption that "pervades the state, from local bureaucrats, [to] traffic police soliciting bribes, to high-level corruption."[14] A 2021 study by AmericasBarometer found that Peru had the highest level of perceived political corruption in the Americas, with "88 percent of Peruvians believing that 'more than half' of politicians are crooked."[15] At the time, Peru's parliament had an approval rating of only 11%, with a nearly 90% disapproval rating.[16] (Nearly the opposite of China!) Further evidence of the political system's dysfunctionality is that, although the president is elected for a five year term, Peru "has seen six presidents in five years."[17] Some of them are in prison after having been removed or resigning.

Pedro Castillo

The sixth president was Pedro Castillo. He was elected in July of 2021, about a year and a half before the demonstrations. He was very popular among the impoverished electorate in part because, as an indigenous person, he made them feel understood, and he promised to work to alleviate the suffering of the poor, reduce inequality, eliminate the corruption, and reform the constitution.

However, his time in office was quite turbulent due to descension in the ranks. He "went through five Cabinets and over 80 ministers in just 17 months."[18]

The parliament was loaded with members of the opposition. They impeached him three times. After the second time, he tried to dissolve that branch of government, but without legal justification. This provided the impetus for the third impeachment, and a vote for removal from office. He was then charged with corruption and jailed pending trial.[19] His supporters saw this removal as an unacceptable attack by the detested

Congress on their chosen leader. Indeed, "44% of Peruvians said they supported Castillo's attempt to dissolve the legislature, even though he tried to do it outside constitutional bounds."[20] The removal and jailing of Castillo was the last straw for his supporters, and they filled the streets.

His Vice President, Dina Boluarte, succeeded him as president. However, she was not trusted by Castillo's supporters. Because they saw her as too cozy with the legislature, they demanded her resignation. They also demanded that Castillo be reinstated, so that his promises could be fulfilled.[21]

The Causal Effect of Poor Performance

This account of the current events in Peru illustrates how political system dysfunction can be the probable cause of extreme political unhappiness, and even hostile political action. Clearly, the political system's dysfunction and the deadly protests are not merely concurrent events. The prior poor governing of the system is most probably responsible for the violent conflict in the streets.

This is not to say that the cause was automatic, or mechanical. The people who protested could have done otherwise. For example, they could have peacefully called their representatives, or written letters, or even lobbied in person. Their decisions to act as they did were the ultimate cause of their behavior, but the long prior history of system dysfunction and abuse, culminating in Castillo's removal and jailing, ignited such resentment and outrage that hundreds of individuals decided to rebel. A chain of system dysfunctions were the *reasons* the people had for acting as they did.

Thomas Jefferson's Testimony

These examples of the causal connection between system function and public attitudes and actions suggest several questions for further research. For example, how much political unhappiness can people tolerate before they protest, rebel, or even revolt?

In general, people tend to have some degree of expectation for the proper performance of their political system. Finding out what those expectations are in particular cases will require research using interpretive methods. These expectations will likely vary from time to time, and from place to place. People also have some degree of tolerance for regimes that fall short of their expectations. What and how much they can tolerate is also a matter for further research.

One well-known meditation on how much dysfunction and abuse a people can tolerate is found in the Declaration of Independence. Its author, Thomas Jefferson wrote,

> Prudence, indeed, will dictate that Governments long established should not be changed for light and transient causes; and accordingly all experience hath shewn, that mankind are more disposed to suffer, while evils are sufferable, than to right themselves by abolishing the forms to which they are accustomed. But when a long train of abuses and usurpations, pursuing invariably the same Object evinces a design to reduce them under absolute Despotism, it is their right, it is their duty, to throw off such Government, and to provide new Guards for their future security. Such has been the patient sufferance of these Colonies; and such is now the necessity which constrains them to alter their former Systems of Government … and to institute new Government, laying its foundation on such principles and organizing its powers in such form, as to them shall

seem most likely to effect their Safety and Happiness.[22]

Jefferson, then, seems to acknowledge that a voluntaristic causal relationship exists between the performance of a political system and the sentience, or political "Happiness," of the people who live within it.

As we have said, what that relationship is will depend on the cases under study. The degree of political frustration a people feel will depend on several factors. The meanings for them that the acts of public officials take is a key factor to consider when assessing their degree of support or hostility towards their system. Their shared meanings are the basis for the decision to act that each individual makes. In contemporary Peru, these shared meanings erupted into overt rebellion. In colonial America, these shared meanings exploded into violent revolution. In both cases, the interpretations the members of the political system made as to the conduct of their governing regime were the reasons for their responses.

The examples of China and Peru illustrate some of the ways by which the performance of a political system will be reflected in the political sentience and behavior of the people who live within the system. The example of China demonstrates that a well-functioning political system will probably engender high approval ratings among its membership. The Peru example shows how a poorly functioning system will probably produce low approval ratings.

The methodology of interpretive political science rises to the level of a "science," in large part, because it has a well-defined set of methods for empirical research, and a clear theory of causal relations, as shown here. That is, *reasons*, empathically interpreted, can serve as a *causal explanation* for political attitudes and behavior.[23]

Not pining for the fantasy ideal of "objectivity," this causal theory only requires the intersubjective agreement of other political scientists to rank claims of causation as "highly probable," or a moderate "possible," or "improbable," or "impossible," etc. The unattainable ideal of "objective" political science knowledge plagues positivist political scientists, and causes them to deny the validity of interpretive methods as ways of research in the field. The dogma that "correlation is not causation" blinds positivists to the rich subtlety of "meaning-links" between political system performance and the attitudes and actions of the people who live in the system.

But interpretive political science can produce claims to knowledge with degrees of certainty that are appropriate to the subject matter – the political behavior of creative human beings who act according to the meanings they currently share within the context of their political system. In short, discovering all the elements of the causal relations between the performance of a political system and the feelings and actions of the people who live in that system is a rich area for further interpretive research.

Part Four: Feelings in Science

Positivism's idea of science is that of strict rationality. All feelings or emotions are to be left outside the laboratory door. But studies of scientist behavior suggest that the positivist views reflect more self-alienation than actual behavioral fact. The scientist/philosopher, Michael Polanyi was, among other things, a pioneer in the study of passions as an integral part of the practice of science. In this ending section of the Conclusion, we will consider some of his insights, after one more word on diagnosis.

The Art of Diagnosis

The *ability* to diagnose the causes of dysfunction and/or political unhappiness includes training and talent. Some professionals may be gifted with the talent while others may lack such abilities. As Easton has suggested, understanding public sentience requires the gift of empathy.

Some people either lack the ability to understand the feelings of others, or have varying degrees of it.[24]

The gift for diagnosing system performance entails a *feel* for the dynamics of a political system. To get the feel for a political system means that one has integrated an image of the operating system in one's mind. Understanding the dynamics of a system is like understanding the personality characteristics of a friend. One might say of a friend, "I can see Bob doing that!" Or "Mary wouldn't do a thing like that." Likewise, "China wouldn't do a thing like that!" (I.e., try to conquer the world militarily.) Or "I can see the government of Peru doing a thing like that." (I.e., disappearing critics, or spending tax money on personal indulgences.)

Of course, having an intuitive feel for a system is not the same as having knowledge of it. Knowledge results from doing the appropriate research. Feel, or having a hunch, can be suggestive for research or hypothesis formation. This is just one of the feelings that play an important part in the practice of science. Science can be full of passion.[25]

Passions in Science

Polanyi writes about the variety of feelings that scientists have had while doing their work. The thrill of taking on a research problem that a person feels she or he can solve is one instance of passion in science. When a research problem is solved, or a discovery made, there can be a release of tension and a joyful feeling. Polanyi says that there is "an elation of a kind which only a scientist can feel and which science alone can evoke in him."[26] As an example he tells the old story of Archimedes rushing naked from his bath into the streets of Syracuse shouting 'Eureka,' after suddenly solving a math problem. And as Kepler wrote, explaining his discovery of the Third Law regarding planetary orbits around the sun, he declared, '...nothing holds me; I will indulge my sacred fury...'[27]

However, writes Polanyi, these are not the only feelings that come from doing science. He says of his great book, *Personal Knowledge*, that "I want to show that scientific passions are no mere psychological by-product, but have a logical function which contributes *an indispensable element to science*."[28] By this he means that, beyond the thrills and joys we mentioned, feelings, or passions, indeed excitement, can be an actual element of the scientific method. This claim is in stark contrast to the positivist vision of the so-called dispassionate, if not self-alienated, rational choice modeler. As we will now see, both Polanyi and Easton make observations about the role of pre-conceptual feelings, passions, and intuitions as these can shed light on the practice of Normative Political Science.

The Passion for Knowing Reality

Polanyi writes that one passion which is general among researchers in the natural sciences is the yearning to bring their understanding of nature closer to reality. Indeed, the passion to know political reality more closely is what drove Easton's critique of Bentley. It's the reason he rejected all forms of equilibrium theory. Those concepts just did not jibe with Easton's pre-conceptual intuitive sense of political reality. Easton recognized the same intuitive feel for the subject matter in other political scientists.

As we mentioned in Chapter 1, Easton admired the political scientist, and leading expert on public opinion studies, V. O. Key, in part, because of his "feel for politics."[29] Also, in Easton's view, those political scientists who have studied "the role of institutions in the political process [have] *instinctively ... felt* that [they are an important] factor shaping policy."[30] Easton complimented Charles Merriam for his "acute political instincts," because Merriam rejected the idea of static equilibrium.[31]

Based on his personal experience in the profession, Easton has observed that "many political scientists" have a "feeling," or "sound instinct," that in the absence of "a common core of knowledge and a unifying framework for all political research," traditional political theory should be studied as "the one field, if any, that can give [the profession] a sense of unity."[32] In the past, even without a unifying field theory, "most students of political life [have felt] quite instinctively" that political science research constitutes "a separate intellectual enterprise" among the social sciences.[33] Also without knowing about Easton's theory of the political system as a rule of relevance, those political scientists with a strong feel for their subject matter agreed "instinctively" that the term "'political' refers to a separate dimension of human activity."[34]

Easton's theory of the political system raises this *feeling,* or intuition, that political science has its own distinct realm of study, to the level of a clear conceptual framework. We have shown how Easton's interpretive framework can help to guide the political science researcher who has a passion to seek a closer understanding of political reality. We have endeavored to show that the ability of Normative Political Science's evaluative methods to rate the performance of political systems is a huge advancement towards satisfying that passion. Using the political system model, political scientists can now know how a system is actually operating, including its below par, or dysfunctional, operations. Just as medical doctors have learned to understand the elements of physical health with models of human wellness, political scientists can now understand the operational goodness of political systems.

This desire for a closer understanding of political reality is why, for many political scientists, including Easton, positivistic methods and assumptions are such a source of frustration. The assumptions of a mechanically "rational" actor, for example, while necessary for mathematical models, are a patent mutilation of the sentient, creative, meaning making human being who engages in political behavior. (However, while not "science," rational choice theory and game theory can be useful to policy makers as a way to clarify options and possible consequences.)

Moral Passion

Another passion Easton has observed among political scientists is the moral, or ethical, motivation some folks have had for studying the subject. In previous chapters we quoted Easton's observation that from its beginning the "inspiration behind political science is clearly ethical." Again, writing in the early 1950s, Easton uses the terms "moral" and "ethical" as interchangeable categories of "value."[35]

Particular moral passions, as we noted earlier, can run the gamut of political philosophies about the "good," or "just," society. Easton was referring to a moral passion in general, which he contrasted with the emotionally dishonest claim of positivists who deny having any moral passion – even as they recoil from criticizing the current regime. Easton urged political scientists to learn to be emotionally honest about their moral motives. Exemplary in this regard are the members of the Caucus for a New Political Science who have always expressed their feeling of being called to use the knowledge of political science to help "make a better world."

The moral passion recognized by Easton, underlies the craving for change that political scientists, such as those in the CNPS, often feel towards their profession, but which crashes against a seemingly unmovable wall of indifference, conceit, and condescension among the more powerful positivist elites. As we have seen, science values are one set of values, moral values are another set of values. Far from being in conflict, they can complement each other. Both Easton and Polanyi recognized that a researcher may have her or his own set of moral values which animates their research, and also have a set of scientific values which keeps their scientific activities in line.

For some political scientists, this moral passion can act as yet another "rule of relevance." In Chapter Five we suggested that a researcher can use his or her political philosophy or ideology as a guide in formulating a research project. Even within the research process such passion will lead the researcher's mind to disregard the information he or she deems useless to the study, cutting through it to find what is needed. In this sense, political science can be steeped in moral passion, yet conducting itself according to the constraints of its scientific method.

Sagely, Polanyi writes, "Theories of the scientific method which try to explain the establishment of scientific truth by any purely objective formal procedure are doomed to failure. Any process of enquiry unguided by intellectual passions would inevitably spread out into a desert of trivialities."[36] Easton said as much when he condemned "hyperfactualism." Today's pages of the APSR are further evidence of the sterility of research pretending to be "value free" and "objective." Indeed, members of the public, as well as political activists and political professionals often criticize the political science profession for its sterility and irrelevance.[37]

Why Adopt Normative Political Science?

Of course, Normative Political Science is a new paradigm, a new interpretive framework. One may legitimately question why the effort should be made to learn it. Polanyi has an answer. He advises his readers that the effort to learn a new point of view can be undertaken "in the hope of attuning our understanding, perception or sensuality more closely to what is true and right."[38] This effort can also be "entered upon in the hope of achieving thereby closer contact with reality."[39] He says that each of us can be like the "innovator and explorer, passionately pouring himself into an existence closer to reality."[40] He adds that this "is a decision, originating in our own personal judgment, to modify … our intellectual existence, so as to become more satisfying to ourselves."[41]

Natural science has proven the ability of Science to find ways to make life better for humanity. The Normative Political Science paradigm sets out the methods by which political science can do the same. For example, once the causes of system malfunction and/or political unhappiness are clearly known, remedies may be proposed in a professional way by applied political science. Those political activists who can recognize political wisdom when they see it will strive to have the wisdom implemented.

The Normative Political Science paradigm now gives our profession an exciting new way by which political science can realize its full potential for both understanding political reality and for using our knowledge to help humanity to live a better life. We need only begin to apply that paradigm to start actualizing our potential.

Endnotes

[1] In reference to Robert K. Merton, Easton writes, "our actions are influenced by the way in which we define a situation." Easton 1953, 1971, p. 26f., 31, 53 n. 20, passim. As mentioned earlier (n. 85., p. 37), Easton was influenced by R. K. Merton, who was influenced by the "symbolic interactionism" of George H. Mead. (One place to search these names for a wealth of references is Wikipedia.) How this social psychology links to the hypothesis that basic political behavior may be influenced by humanity's self-bred genome, as alluded to in Chapter Two, has yet to be sorted out. There are still difficult questions like, "Why does political behavior exist?" Or, "Why has political behavior, that behavior in relation to a political system, existed throughout human history?" Or, "Why does political behavior appear to exist among all human societies on Earth today?" My evolutionary explanation, posited in Chapter Two, begins to address these questions.

[2] The mechanical theory for the causation of political behavior also reduces the stature, or value, of the human subjects to that of mechanically acting devices, like robots or machines. But the causal theory offered here honors the humanity of political actors by acknowledging their creative capacity for meaning making, and their autonomy and responsibility, at least in part, for their meanings and behavior. (Cf. Note 1, above.) Whether the reduction of human value to that of things, implied in the work of positivist political science, has had any influence

on public opinion towards the political science profession is a matter yet to be fully researched. Cf., n. 37, below.

3. Generally, "public opinion" consists of individuals forming, or creating, opinions or suspicions or hunches about government behavior, each in her or his own mind. This self-formation of meanings is a kind of interpretation of government behavior. Cf. note 1, above.

4. As we have said, each individual creates her or his own meanings, using the clues of experience, and the materials of education and socialization. Because these individual sets of meanings overlap, meaningful statements about group ideologies, or larger cultures, are possible. See Polanyi 1958. This is similar to Wittgenstein's notion of "family resemblances."

5. While the terms "cause" or "causation" can be used, various non-mechanistic meanings can be implied. A non-mechanistic meaning for the term "cause" can include variations on the word "prompt," such as give rise to, bring about, occasion, result in, lead to, elicit, produce, bring on, engender, induce, call forth, evoke, precipitate, trigger, spark off, provoke, instigate, and so on. Using these meanings, a researcher might ask, for example, do the operations of the political system *cause* the meanings and feelings that the members have toward it? If so, how does the system cause the meanings? Or does the public independently *interpret* the meanings of system operations?

6. Polanyi 1958. The idea that knowing always contains uncertainty is central to his critique of positivism throughout the book. Since the term "hazardous knowing" is not in the index, some suggestive pages are 93, 115,and Chapter Two, esp. sec. 6 passim. Polanyi's writings on the social psychology of science and knowledge can be fully understood and appreciated without accepting his comments on religion.

7. While an interesting notion upon which to speculate, deciding whether or not constructive political behavior has a genetic cause is a matter outside the parameters of political science.

8. While widely written about, I have discussed some of the reasons for the Chinese Economic Miracle in Chapter Four. The policy of Common Prosperity reflects an interesting effort by Chinese thinkers to synthesize Confucianism and Marxism. See for example Yang, Y. 2023.

9. With 50 Dead in Peru, a Referendum on Democracy. By Julie Turkewitz. The New York Times. Published Jan. 17, 2023.
https://www.nytimes.com/2023/01/17/world/americas/peru-protests-democracy.html?searchResultPosition=2

10. The Real Reason Behind Peru's Political Crisis. By Simeon Tegel. Foreign Policy Magazine. January 25, 2023

https://foreignpolicy.com/2023/01/25/peru-protests-political-crisis-castillo-boluarte-corruption/

COVID death rate per 100,000 population. Johns Hopkins University. February 4, 2023

https://coronavirus.jhu.edu/data/mortality.

Also see, Peru revises pandemic death toll, now worst in the world per capita. By Marco Aquino and Marcelo Rochabrun. May 31, 2021

https://www.reuters.com/world/americas/peru-almost-triples-official-covid-19-death-toll-after-review-180000-2021-05-31/ (Also using Johns Hopkins numbers)

[12.] Tegel 2023, cf. n. 10.

[13.] Ibid.

[14.] Ibid.

[15.] Ibid.

[16.] Peru's president to replace prime minister in Cabinet shakeup. By Marco Aquino. December 18, 2022

https://www.reuters.com/world/americas/peru-president-says-she-will-replace-prime-minister-2022-12-19/

[17.] Peru's 'forgotten people' rage against political elite after Castillo arrest. By Alexander Villegas and Marco Aquino. December 18, 2022

https://www.reuters.com/world/americas/perus-forgotten-people-rage-against-political-elite-after-castillo-arrest-2022-12-18/

[18.] Ibid.

[19.] Ibid.

[20.] Ibid.

[21.] Peru: growing outrage over protest deaths as president urged to resign. Dan Collyns. Jan 19, 2023

https://www.theguardian.com/world/2023/jan/19/peru-lima-president-protests-clashes. Cf. Villegas, supra.

[22.] Declaration of Independence at,

https://www.archives.gov/founding-docs/declaration-transcript.

[23.] A compelling argument for using reasons in non-mechanistic causal explanations can be found in Michael Polanyi. *The Study of Man* (1958). The University of Chicago Press, Chicago, Ill. Especially pp. 90-93.

[24.] Whether the gifts of empathy and those mathematical gifts prized by positivists can exist in the same mind or not is a question best left to social psychologists to answer.

[25.] This feel for the system can also play a part in the validation process. That a claim to knowledge doesn't feel right can be an impetus to do some counter research, or to withhold judgment until more facts are known. Perhaps the main part of validating the results of research is the critical examination of the methods used, and of the inferences drawn therefrom.

[26.] Polanyi 1958, p134

[27.] Ibid., full quote at p. 7.

[28.] Ibid.

[29.] Easton 1953, 1971, p144, n12.

[30.] Ibid., 152, emp. ad.

[31.] Ibid., 279.

[32.] Ibid., 308-309.

[33.] Ibid., 96.

[34.] Ibid., 99.

[35.] Ibid. p. 223. Perhaps since Easton's time the two terms have been gravitating apart; "ethical" moving more towards specific forms of behavior, as in "business ethics," and "moral" more towards broader principles of ideological conduct, e.g., from conservative to radical. Easton intended the latter meaning.

[36.] Polanyi, ibid., p135.

[37.] See, Does Political Science Force Graduate Students into a Career of Irrelevancy? Kelleher, William. November 6, 2020. https://interpretat.blogspot.com/2020/11/does-political-science-force-graduate.html

[38.] Polanyi, ibid., p. 106.

[39.] Ibid.

[40.] Ibid. p335.

[41.] Ibid. p.106.

References

A

APSA Constitution.
https://www.apsanet.org/portals/54/Files/APASConstitution2011.pdf
Ardrey, Robert. 1961, 2014. *African Genesis*. New York: StoryDesign LTD
______. 2014. *The Hunting Hypothesis*. New York: StoryDesign LTD.
______. 1996, 1997. *The Territorial Imperative*. New York: Kodansha America.
Aquino, Marco and Marcelo Rochabrun. 2021. "Peru revises pandemic death toll, now worst in the world per capita." *Reuters.* May 31, 2021.
https://www.reuters.com/world/americas/peru-almost-triples-official-covid-19-death-toll-after-review-180000-2021-05-31/_____(Also using Johns Hopkins numbers)
______. 2022. "Peru's president to replace prime minister in Cabinet shakeup." *Reuters.* December 18, 2022.
https://www.reuters.com/world/americas/peru-president-says-she-will-replace-prime-minister-2022-12-19/.
Aronoff, Myron J, Jan Kubik. 2013. *Anthropology and Political Science: A Convergent Approach*. New York: Berghahn Books.

B

Barkow, Jerome H., Leda Cosmides, and John Tooby. 1992. *The Adapted Mind: Evolutionary Psychology and the Generation of Culture.* New York: Oxford University Press.
Barton, N.H. 2006. "Evolutionary Biology: How Did the Human Species Form?" *Dispatch* 16(16): PR647-R650.
doi.org/10.1016/j.cub.2006.07.032
Bekoff, Marc. 2013. "A Universal Declaration on Animal Sentience." *Psychology Today Online*
https://www.psychologytoday.com/blog/animal-emotions/201306/universal-declaration-animal-sentience-no-pretending Retrieved May 30, 2020
Binford, Lewis. 1981, 2014. *Bones: Ancient Men and Modern Myths*. Cambridge, MA: Academic Press.

______. 1985. "Human Ancestors: Changing Views of their Behavior." *Journal of Anthropology and Archeology* 4:292–327.

Boehm, Christopher. 1993. "Egalitarian Behavior and Reverse Dominance Hierarchy." Current Anthropology 34(3):227–254.

Bergson, Henri. 1907. *Creative Evolution.*

Brown, K., Bērziņa-Čerenkova, U.A.2018. "Ideology in the Era of Xi Jinping." *Journal of Chinese Political Science* 23, 323–339. https://doi.org/10.1007/s11366-018-9541-z

Brown, Kerry. 2012. "The Communist Party of China and Ideology." *China: An International Journal.* 10 (2). National University of Singapore Press.

C

Callaway, Ewen. 2017. "Oldest Homo sapiens fossil claim rewrites our species' history." *Nature* doi:10.1038/nature.2017.22114

Chang, Hasok. 2004. *Inventing Temperature: Measurement and Scientific Progress.* Oxford University Press, USA.

Clissold, Tim. 2004. *Mr. China.* Robinson, UK.

Collyns, Dan. 2023. "Peru: growing outrage over protest deaths as president urged to resign." *The Guardian.* Jan 19, 2023 https://www.theguardian.com/world/2023/jan/19/peru-lima-president-protests-clashes.

D

Darwin, Charles. 1859. *The Origin of Species by Means of Natural Selection*, 6th Edition. London: John Murray.

______. 1871. *The Descent of Man, and Selection in Relation to Sex.* London: John Murray.

Declaration of Independence National Archives. https://www.archives.gov/founding-docs/declaration-transcript.

de Waal, Frans. 1996. *Good Natured: The Origins of Right and Wrong in Humans and Other Animals.* Cambridge, MA: Harvard University Press.

______. 1998. *Chimpanzee Politics: Sex and Power among the* Apes. Baltimore: Johns Hopkins University Press.

______. (ed.) 2002. *Tree of Origin: What Primate Behavior Can Tell Us about Human Social Evolution*. Cambridge: Harvard University Press.

Diamant, Neil J. 2022. *Useful Bullshit: Constitutions in Chinese Politics and Society.* Cornell University Press.

E

Easton, David. 1965a. *A Framework for Political Analysis.* New Jersey: Prentice-Hall.

______. 1965b. *A Systems Analysis of Political Life.* New York: John Wiley & Sons

______. "Political Anthropology." 1959. In *Biennial Review of Anthropology*. Bernard Siegel (ed). Stanford: Stanford University Press 1959 https://archive.org/stream/biennialreviewof033489mbp/biennialreview of033489mbp_djvu.txt

______. 1953. *The Political System.* New York: Alfred A. Knopf, Inc.

F

Fisher, Ronald A. 1930. *The Genetical Theory of Natural Selection*. Oxford: Clarendon Press.

Flannery, Kent and Joyce Marcus. 2012. *The Creation of Inequality: How Our Prehistoric Ancestors Set the Stage for Monarchy, Slavery, and Empire*. Cambridge: Harvard University Press.

Fried, Morton H., *The Evolution of Political Society: An Essay in Political Anthropology* (New York: Random House, 1967).

Fromm, Erich. 1961. *Marx's Conception of Man.* Frederick Ungar Publishing: New York. In pdf at, https://www.marxists.org/archive/fromm/works/1961/man/

G

Gandhi, Jennifer; Noble, Ben; Svolik, Milan. 2020. "Legislatures and Legislative Politics Without Democracy." *Comparative Political Studies.* 53 (9): 1359–1379. doi:10.1177/0010414020919930

Geertz, Clifford. 1962. *The Growth of Culture and the Evolution of Mind.* Glencoe: Free Press.

Gintis, Herbert. 2000. "Strong Reciprocity and Human Sociality." *Journal of Theoretical Biology* 206:169–179.

______. 2003. "The Hitchhiker's Guide to Altruism: Genes, Culture, and the Internalization of Norms." *Journal of Theoretical Biology* 220(4):407–418.
Gintis, Herbert, Carel van Schaik and Christopher Boehm. 2019.
______. "Zoon Politikon: The Evolutionary Origins of Human Socio-political Systems." *Behavioural Processes* 161:17-30.
 doi.org/10.1016/j.beproc.2018.01.007
Godley, Michael R. 1987. "Socialism with Chinese Characteristics: Sun Yatsen and the International Development of China". *The Australian Journal of Chinese Affairs* (18): 109–125. doi:10.2307/2158585.
Gowlett, John A. J. and Richard W. Wrangham. 2013. "Earliest Fire in Africa: Towards the Convergence of Archaeological Evidence and the Cooking Hypothesis." *Azania: Archaeological Research in Africa* 48(1): 5-30.
Gowlett, J.A.J. 2016. "The discovery of fire by humans: a long and convoluted process." *Phil. Trans. R. Soc.* B 371: 1-12. doi.org/10.1098/rstb.2015.0164

H
Harsha, Dan. 2020. "Taking China's Pulse: Ash Center research team unveils findings from long-term public opinion survey.". *Ash Center Communications*. July 9, 2020.
https://news.harvard.edu/gazette/story/2020/07/long-term-survey-reveals-chinese-government-satisfaction/
Hartman, Robert. 1967. *The Structure of Value: Foundations of Scientific Axiology*. Carbondale and Edwardsville, Ill.: Southern Illinois University Press, 1967.
______. 2002. *The Knowledge of Good: Critique of Axiological Reason*. Brill Rodopi; 2002. Free download at,
 https://www.hartmaninstitute.org/additional-axiology-books
______. 1959. "The Scientific Basis of Value Theory." In *New Knowledge in Human Values*, ed. Abraham H. Maslow. New York: Harper, 1959.
______. 1958. "Value, Fact, and Science," Philosophy of Science, 25 (April 1958), pp. 97- 108.
Heilmann, Sebastian. 2017. *China's Political System*. Rowman & Littlefield, London.
Holmes, Oliver Wendell. 1917. Dissenting opinion in Southern Pacific *Company v. Jensen*, 244 U.S. 205, 222 (1917) that "[t]he common law is

not a brooding omnipresence in the sky, but the articulate voice of some sovereign or quasi sovereign that can be identified."

I

Isaac, Barbara (ed). 1989. *The Archaeology of Human Origins: Papers by Glynn Isaac*. Cambridge: Cambridge University Press.
Isaac, Glynn. 1978. "The Food-sharing Behavior of Protohuman Hominids," *Scientific American* 238(4): 90–108.
 doi:10.1038/scientificamerican0478-90.
_____. 1978. "Food Sharing and Human Evolution." *Journal of Anthropological Research* 34(3): 311-325.

J

Johns Hopkins University. 2023. "COVID death rate per 100,000 population." February 4 ,2023.
https://coronavirus.jhu.edu/data/mortality.

K

Kelleher, William J. (2017) "Back to the Future: How Understanding David Easton Can Give Guidance to the Caucus for a New Political Science." New Political Science (2017) 39 (4): 473–486.
https://doi.org/10.1080/07393148.2017.1378293
_____. 2016. "Can Chimpanzee Politics Constitute a Political System?" https://www.academia.edu/20299604/Can_Chimpanzee_Politics_Const itute_a_Political_System
_____. 2020. "Does Political Science Force Graduate Students into a Career of Irrelevancy?" November 06, 2020.
 https://interpretat.blogspot.com/2020/11/does-political-science-force-graduate.html
_____. 2017. "Letting Easton Be Easton—An Interpretivist." *Qualitative & Multi-Method Research* 15(2)
 doi.org/10.5281/zenodo.2563168
_____. 2021. "Normative Political Science – How to Measure the Goodness of a Political System." APSA Preprints.
https://preprints.apsanet.org/engage/apsa/article-details/610077128804435530e40d32

______. 2020. "The Origins of Political Behavior, and the First Political System." APSA Preprints. https://preprints.apsanet.org/engage/apsa/article-details/5f4817b9572c8200124a3cdd

______. 2009. "Respect and Empathy in the Social Science Writings of Michael Polanyi." *Tradition and Discovery: The Polanyi Society Periodical.* 35 (1), pp. 8-32. DOI: 10.5840/traddisc20083515.

King, Andrew et al. 2009. "The Origins and Evolution of Leadership." *Current Biology* 19: R911–R916. doi.org/10.1016/j.cub.2009.07.027

Lasswell, Harlod. 1936. *Politics, Who gets What, When, and How.*

Kuhn, Thomas. 1962, 1970. *The Structure of Scientific Revolutions.* University of Chicago Press.

L

Leakey, Mary. 1971. *Olduvai Gorge, Excavations in Beds I and III, 1960–1963*, Vol. 3 Cambridge: Cambridge University Press.

Leakey, Richard E. and Roger Lewin. 1979. *People of the Lake: Mankind & Its Beginnings.* New York: Avon Books.

Low, Philip et al. 2012. *The Cambridge Declaration on Consciousness.* http://fcmconference.org/img/CambridgeDeclarationOnConsciousness.pdf

Lumsden, Charles J. and Edward O. Wilson. 1981. *Genes, Mind, and Culture: The Coevolutionary Process.* Cambridge, MA: Harvard University Press.

Lü, Xiaobo; Liu, Mingxing; Li, Feiyue. 2020. "Policy Coalition Building in an Authoritarian Legislature: Evidence From China's National Assemblies (1983-2007)." *Comparative Political Studies.* 53 (9): 1380–1416. doi:10.1177/0010414018797950

M

Miller, Alice. 2010. "The 18th Central Committee Politburo: A Quixotic, Foolhardy, Rashly Speculative, But Nonetheless Ruthlessly Reasoned Projection." *China Leadership Monitor.* https://media.hoover.org/sites/default/files/documents/CLM33AM.pdf

Mithen, Steven. 1991. "Home Bases and Stone Caches: The Archaeology of Early Hominid Activities." *Cambridge Archaeological Journal* 1(02): 277-283. doi:10.1017/s095977430000041x

Morris, Desmond. 1967, 1999. *The Naked Ape*. New York: Delta.

Nengo, I., et al. 2017. "New infant cranium from the African Miocene sheds light on ape evolution." *Nature* 548: 169–174. doi.org/10.1038/nature23456

N

O

O'Connell, James F., Kristen Hawkes, et al. 2002. "Male Strategies and Plio-Pleistocene Archaeology," *Journal of Human Evolution* 43(6):831–872. doi.org/10.1006/jhev.2002.0604

P

Pagel, Mark. 2012. *Wired for Culture*. New York: W. W. Norton.

Parenti, Michael. 1974. *Democracy for the Few* (1974).

Patterson, Nick et al. 2006. "Genetic evidence for complex speciation of humans and chimpanzees." *Nature* 441(7097): 1103-1108. doi:10.1038/nature04789.

Perry, E. 2015. "The Populist Dream of Chinese Democracy." *The Journal of Asian Studies*. 74(4), 903-915. doi:10.1017/S0021911815000114X https://www.cambridge.org/core/journals/journal-of-asian-studies/article/populist-dream-of-chinese-democracy/9DD98A6858F2808B0E2D3BE3964481A1

Pieke, Frank N. 2009. *The Good Communist: Elite Training and State Building in Today's China*. Cambridge: Cambridge University Press.

______. 2016. *Knowing China*. Cambridge University Press. https://doi.org/10.1017/CBO9781316452097

Pinker, Steven. 2010. "The Cognitive Niche: Coevolution of Intelligence, Sociality and Language." *Proceedings of the National Academy of Sciences* 107(2):8993–8999.

Polanyi, Michael. 1958, 1962, 1964. *Personal Knowledge. Towards a Post-Critical Philosophy*. Harper, NY.

______. 1958. *The Study of Man*. The University of Chicago Press, Chicago, Ill. (Especially pp. 90-93.)

Pomiankowski, Andrew N. 1987. "The Costs of Choice in Sexual Selection," *Journal of Theoretical Biology* 128:195–218.

Potts, Richard. 1984. "Home Bases and Early Hominids: Reevaluation of the fossil record at Olduvai Gorge." *American Scientist* 72(4): 338-347.

______. 1988. *Early Hominid Activities at Olduvai Gorge.* New York: Aldine de Gruyter.

Q

R

Richerson, Peter J. and Robert Boyd. 2004. *Not by Genes Alone.* Chicago: University of Chicago Press.

Rodrik, Dani. 1997. "The Paradoxes of the Successful State.*" European Economic Review.* 41 (3–5): 411–442. https://doi.org/10.1016/S0014-2921(97)00012-3

Roebroeks, W. and P. Villa. 2011. "On the Earliest Evidence for Habitual Use of Fire in Europe." *Proceedings of the National Academy of Sciences* 108: 5209–5214.

Rolland, Nicolas. 2004. "Was the Emergence of Home Bases and Domestic Fire a Punctuated Event?" *Asian Perspectives* 43(2): 248-280. doi:10.1353/asi.2004.0027

S

Samuelson, Robert. 1967. "Political Science: CIA, Ethics Stir Otherwise Placid Convention." Science New Series, Vol. 157, No. 3795 (Sep. 22, 1967), pp. 1414-1417

Schwartz-Shea, Peregrine. 2014. "Judging Quality Evaluative Criteria and Epistemic Communities," Chapter Seven, 120-146. In Yanow, Dvora and Peregrine Schwartz-Shea. *Interpretation and Method Empirical Research Methods and the Interpretive Turn.* 2nd Edition. 2014. M. E. Sharpe, NY.

Service, E. R. 1975. *Origin of the State and Civilization: The Process of Cultural Evolution.* New York: Norton.

Shambaugh, David. 2008. *China's Communist Party: Atrophy and Adaptation.* University of California Press, Berkeley.

Shum, Desmond. 2021. *Red Roulette: An Insider's Story of Wealth, Power, Corruption, and Vengeance in Today's China*. Simon & Schuster, UK.

Smith, Cyril. 1996. *Marx At the Millennium.* Pluto Press: UK. In pdf at, https://www.marxists.org/reference/archive/smith-cyril/works/millenni/index.htm

Snow, Edgar. 1937, 1961. *Red Star Over China*. New York, NY.

Stiner, M. C. 2002. "Carnivory, Coevolution, and the Geographic Spread of the genus Homo." *Journal of Archeological Research* 10:1–63.

Stiner, M. C., R. Barkai, and A. Gopher. 2009. "Cooperative Hunting and Meat Sharing." *Proceedings of the National Academy of Sciences* 106 (32): 13207–13212.

Surkine, M., & Wolfe, A. 1970. "The Political Dimension of American Political Science." Acta Politica, 5: 1969/1970(1), 43-61. Retrieved from https://hdl.handle.net/1887/3451185

T

Tegel, Simeon. 2023. "The Real Reason Behind Peru's Political Crisis." *Foreign Policy Magazine*. January 25, 2023. https://foreignpolicy.com/2023/01/25/peru-protests-political-crisis-castillo-boluarte-corruption/

Truex, Rory. 2016. *Making Autocracy Work: Representation and Responsiveness in Modern China*. Cambridge: Cambridge University Press.

Turkewitz, Julie. 2023. "With 50 Dead in Peru, a Referendum on Democracy." *The New York Times*. Published Jan. 17, 2023. https://www.nytimes.com/2023/01/17/world/americas/peru-protests-democracy.html?searchResultPosition=2

U

V

Valentini, Giacomo. 2021. "China's Common Prosperity Drive." Internationalisms. Blogspot. Posted December 29, 202.1 https://internationalisms.blogspot.com/2021/12/chinas-common-prosperity-drive-us.html.

Villegas, Alexander and Marco Aquino. 2022. "Peru's 'forgotten people' rage against political elite after Castillo arrest." By December 18, 2022 https://www.reuters.com/world/americas/perus-forgotten-people-rage-against-political-elite-after-castillo-arrest-2022-12-18/

von Rueden, C. et al. 2014. "Leadership in an Egalitarian Society." *Human Nature* 25(4): 538–566. doi.org/10.1007/s12110-014-9213-4

W

Wallace, Jeremy L. 2016. "Juking the Stats? Authoritarian Information Problems in China." *British Journal of Political Science*. 46 (1): 11–29. doi:10.1017/S0007123414000106.

Whallon, Robert. 1989. "The Human Revolution." In P. Mellars and C. Stringer (eds.) *The Human Revolution: Behavioral and Biological Perspectives on the Origins of Modern Humans*. Princeton: Princeton University Press.

Wiessner, Polly. 2008. "The Power of One? The Big Man Revisited." In Kevin J. Vaugh (ed.) *The Evolution of Leadership: Transitions in Decision Making*. Santa Fe: SAR Press.

Wike, Richard and Bruce Stokes. 2016. "Chinese Public Sees More Powerful Role in World, Names U.S. as Top Threat." *Pew Research Center Report*. October 5, 2016. https://www.pewresearch.org/global/2016/10/05/chinese-public-sees-more-powerful-role-in-world-names-u-s-as-top-threat/

Wilson, Edward O. 1975. *Sociobiology: The New Synthesis*. Cambridge, MA: Harvard University Press.

______. 2012. *The Social Conquest of Earth*. New York: W.W. Norton.

Wrangham, Richard. 2009. *Catching fire: How cooking made us human*. New York: Basic Books.

______. 2017. "Control of Fire in the Paleolithic: Evaluating the Cooking Hypothesis." *Current Anthropology* 58(S16): S303-S313. doi/full/10.1086/692113

Wrangham, Richard and Dale Peterson. 1996. *Demonic Males: Apes and the Origins of Human Violence*. New York: Mariner Books.

Wrangham, Richard and Rachel Carmody. 2010. "Human Adaptation to the Control of Fire." *Evolutionary Anthropology* 19:187–199.

Wu, Guoguang. 2015. *China's Party Congress: Power, Legitimacy, and Institutional Manipulation*. Cambridge University Press.

X

Yang, Benjamin. 1990, 2021. *From Revolution to Politics: Chinese Communists on the Long March*. Taylor & Francis, NY.

Y

Yanow, Dvora. 2014. "Neither Rigorous nor Objective? Interrogating Criteria for knowledge Claims in Interpretive Science," Chapter Six, 97-119, *Interpretation and Methods*, op cit.

Z

Zang L. 2022. "Middle Class and Its Attitude Toward Government in Different Political Systems: A Comparison of China and Japan." Chinese Political Science Review (2020) 5(1) 74-94 Section 3.1 (page number not available online) DOI: 10.1007/s41111-018-0115-1

Zhang, Chunhou. Vaughan, C. Edwin. 2002. *Mao Zedong as Poet and Revolutionary Leader: Social and Historical Perspectives*. Lexington books. ISBN 0-7391-0406-3. p. 65.

Zhong, Yan. 2018. "The Theory, Practice, and Institutional Basis for Adding 'The defining feature of socialism with Chinese characteristics is the *leadership* of the Communist Party of China' to the Constitution." People's Daily. Xinhua News Agency. February 28, 2018. http://www.xinhuanet.com/politics/2018-02/28/c_1122465517.htm

Zinn, Howard. 1980. *A People's History of the United States*. Harper Perennial Modern Classics.

Index

20th century, 18
1000 years

A

Ad Hoc Committee on Membership
Revocation, 10
American Political Science Association,
40, 72, 110, 115, 167, 181
American political science profession,
14, 111
APSA, 7, 10, 15, 72, 115, 167, 168, 169,
170, 172, 181, 182, 185, 186, 187,
188, 189, 190, 218, 222, 223
APSA Ethics Committee, 10
Axiom, 4, 17, 22, 24, 27

B

Bayet, 12
behavioral political system, 13, 32, 33,
80, 83, 84, 85, 87, 88, 91, 92, 93, 94,
97, 98, 99, 101, 102, 103, 104, 106,
108, 109, 110, 114, 189
behavioralism, 27, 32, 34, 112, 171,
175, 180, 186
behavioralist, 18, 27, 38
below par, 14, 118, 192, 195, 200, 210
biology,, 19

C

Caucus for a New Political Science, 37,
167, 211
cause, 91, 98, 134, 137, 146, 193, 194,
198, 199, 202, 204, 214
caused interpretation, 198
causes, 14, 32, 77, 102, 110, 118, 139,
149, 156, 177, 183, 192, 193, 195,
197, 200, 205, 207, 213
CCP, 7, 120, 121, 124, 125, 126, 127,
128, 129, 131, 132, 133, 134, 135,
136, 137, 140, 141, 142, 143, 144,
145, 147, 148, 149, 157, 158, 159,
160, 161, 162
chemistry, 19
chimpanzee, 36, 44, 47, 49, 66, 219
China, 6, 7, 8, 33, 41, 62, 63, 104, 111,
112, 118, 119, 120, 121, 122, 124,
127, 130, 132, 133, 135, 136, 137,
139, 140, 141, 142, 143, 144, 145,
146, 147, 148, 149, 150, 152, 153,
154, 156, 157, 158, 159, 160, 161,
162, 163, 201, 202, 203, 206, 208,
219, 221, 223, 224, 225, 226, 227,
228
China's political system, 104, 119, 130,
159
Chinese, 6, 7, 14, 111, 115, 118, 119,
120, 122, 124, 126, 127, 128, 129,

P